P9-EEL-901

The Reward and Recognition Process in Total Quality Management

Also available from ASQC Quality Press

Managing the Four Stages of TQM: How to Achieve World-Class Performance
Charles N. Weaver

Performance-Based Assessments: External, Internal, and Self-Assessment Tools for Total Quality Management
Paul F. Wilson and Richard D. Pearson

Small Business Success Through TQM: Practical Methods to Improve Your Organization's Performance
Terry Ehresman

Show Me: The Complete Guide to Storyboarding and Problem Solving
(workbook also available)
Harry I. Forsha

A World of Quality: The Timeless Passport
Xerox Quality Solutions

The ASQC Total Quality Management Series

> *TQM: Leadership for the Quality Transformation*
> Richard S. Johnson
>
> *TQM: Management Processes for Quality Operations*
> Richard S. Johnson
>
> *TQM: The Mechanics of Quality Processes*
> Richard S. Johnson and Lawrence E. Kazense
>
> *TQM: Quality Training Practices*
> Richard S. Johnson

To request a complimentary catalog of publications, call 800-248-1946.

AMERICAN SOCIETY FOR INDUSTRIAL SECURITY
1625 PRINCE STREET
ALEXANDRIA, VA 22314
(703) 519-6200

HD
62.15
K72
1995

The Reward and Recognition Process in Total Quality Management

Stephen B. Knouse

ASQC Quality Press
Milwaukee, Wisconsin

The Reward and Recognition Process in Total Quality Management
Stephen B. Knouse

Library of Congress Cataloging-in-Publication Data

Knouse, Stephen B.
 The reward and recognition process in total quality management /
 Stephen B. Knouse
  p. cm.
 Includes bibliographical references and index.
 ISBN 0-87389-306-9
 1. Total quality management. 2. Reward (Psychology)
3. Motivation (Psychology) I. Title.
HD62.15.K6 1995
658.5'62—dc20

94-36137
CIP

© 1995 by ASQC

All rights reserved. No part of this book may be reproduced in any form or by any means, electronic, mechanical, photocopying, recording, or otherwise, without the prior written permission of the publisher.

10 9 8 7 6 5 4 3 2 1

ISBN 0-87389-306-9

Acquisitions Editor: Susan Westergard
Project Editor: Kelley Cardinal
Production Editor: Annette Wall
Marketing Administrator: Mark Olson
Set in Galliard by Precision Graphics.
Cover design by Artistic License.
Printed and bound by BookCrafters, Inc.

ASQC Mission: To facilitate continuous improvement and increase customer satisfaction by identifying, communicating, and promoting the use of quality principles, concepts, and technologies; and thereby be recognized throughout the world as the leading authority on, and champion for, quality.

For a free copy of the ASQC Quality Press Publications Catalog, including ASQC membership information, call 800-248-1946.

Printed in the United States of America

  Printed on acid-free recycled paper

 ASQC
Quality Press
611 East Wisconsin Avenue
Milwaukee, Wisconsin 53202

To Teri

Contents

Illustrations

Preface

In the last few years there have been more than a thousand articles published on total quality management (TQM), according to the *Business Periodicals Index*. If you cross-reference *reward and recognition* with *TQM,* you will find that a number of these articles mention the importance of reward and recognition for TQM to succeed. Yet, surprisingly, there is no book on the reward and recognition process, to my knowledge.

Why is there no such book when there definitely seems to be a demand for it? One reason may be that TQM has evolved mainly in manufacturing, a field that has been dominated by engineers such as W. Edwards Deming. Perhaps reflecting their hard science background, they tend to see employee motivation either as something as direct as money or as aesthetic as pride in work. In the former case we already have economic theory to explain how employees relate to money, while in the latter case pride in work is seen by many as highly personal and subjective. As long as we recognize in our gut what Deming is talking about, we understand motivation. But do we really?

This vague approach to concepts like pride in work points out a basic gap in the progress of TQM. There is relatively little psychological theory underlying the understanding of TQM processes in spite of its emphasis on important psychological concepts like cultural change, leadership, and teamwork.

This book attempts to provide psychological frameworks for understanding the reward and recognition process. At the same time I realize that TQM has largely evolved on the practitioner side of the discipline of management. Unfortunately, academics have largely ignored how their theories and concepts would fit into TQM. Therefore, in every chapter I emphasize good practices for improving the reward and recognition process.

Because this is one of the first books in this area, I do not expect it to be able to provide all the answers. I have tried to emphasize diversity and innovation throughout the book. I am addressing reward and recognition not as a static set of principles, but rather as a continually evolving process that must expand into new areas—motivation, leadership, group dynamics, and other areas of the behavioral sciences—if TQM is to be responsive to both its internal customers (employees) and its external customers.

Acknowledgments

I have been privileged to work on TQM projects for several years with the Navy Personnel Research and Development Center (NPRDC), which has been at the forefront of total quality for the Navy (see Mary Walton, *Deming Management at Work*, New York: Putnam, 1990). I learned much from working with several of NPRDC's TQM researchers—Laurie Broedling, Linda Doherty, Steve Dockstader, Del Nebeker, and Mike White. Moreover, in 1992 several events came together propitiously that allowed me to study TQM in Melbourne, Australia. I learned a unique international slant on TQM from several Aussie quality managers—Doug Rutherford of Ford of Australia, Nand Dureja of Amdahl Australia, John Pederson of Broken Hill Proprietary (BHP); David Gaffney of Imperial Chemical Industries (ICI); Bill Fenner, former director of the Australian Quality Circles Association; and Norbert Vogel, director of the Australian Quality Council. In addition, I wish to thank the members of the TQM research unit of Monash University, especially Amrik Sohal, Hans Eisen, and Stuart Orr, for their assistance.

Of course, I must acknowledge the tremendous influence of the leaders of the TQM movement—Philip B. Crosby, J. M. Juran, and especially W. Edwards Deming. (I prefer the term *leader* which implies a teacher, role model, and guide to the popular epithet for these men of *guru* which to me implies something mystic and religious. I believe that TQM is a set of values, not a religion.)

I would like to thank the editorial team at ASQC, especially Susan Westergard, Kelley Cardinal, and Shannon Eglinton. I must also thank my dean, Jan Duggar, and my department head, Bill Roe, for their logistical support. Finally, I must thank my wife and life companion, Teri, for her understanding, tolerance, and patience while I was writing this book.

Chapter 1

Introduction to Total Quality Management

Give the worker a chance to work with pride
         —W. Edwards Deming, *Out of the Crisis*

The recognition step of the quality improvement process is one of its most important.
         —Philip B. Crosby, *Quality Is Free*

Total quality management (TQM) is a significant force in U.S. management. Some believe it is causing a revolutionary change in management thinking—wrenching U.S. managers from a traditional emphasis on producing quantity regardless of quality and then dumping the low-quality products and services on increasingly hostile consumers. In such an environment employees are insulated from the customers' demands for quality and improvement and instead focus inwardly on winning bonuses and awards that attest to their own career accomplishments. In contrast, TQM creates a whole new set of values for the corporation, emphasizing the understanding of consumer desires first and then producing high-quality goods and services to meet those demands. In this environment worker teams strive to continuously improve their products or services to meet constantly changing customer demands. Their rewards are customer praise for a job well-done and recognition from the company for quality improvements.

Others believe that TQM is not so revolutionary but represents a return to earlier American values of craftsmanship where workers were not isolated from the customer but rather worked closely with the customer to produce something that the customer valued and the craftsperson was proud of.[1] Indeed, the craftsperson was proud enough of the work to put his or her craft mark on the product.

1

The purpose of this book is to explore this important motivational aspect of TQM that deals with the reward and recognition process. But, first, we must examine several of the concepts of TQM in order to set the stage for understanding the reward and recognition component.

DEFINITION OF TQM

First we will look at a definition of TQM. There are many approaches to defining TQM. A sampling of several definitions follows. The first is an academic definition.

TQM means that the organization's culture is defined by and supports the constant attainment of customer satisfaction through an integrated system of tools, techniques, and training. This involves the continuous improvement of organizational processes, resulting in high-quality products and services.[2]

The second is a consultant's definition.

TQM is a method of managing and operating a business that seeks to maximize firm value through a practice of maximizing customer satisfaction at the lowest possible cost. Maximizing customer satisfaction at the lowest possible cost is achieved through a focus on continuous improvement of all processes existing within a company, where employees are empowered to improve these processes.[3]

The third is a hospital's definition.

TQM is a systematic approach to implementing lasting change in an organization through the use of teamwork and participation, statistical methods and analysis, management leadership, and problem solving and process management.[4]

And, finally, the fourth is an executive's definition taken from an interview with Edwin Artzt, chief executive officer (CEO) of Procter and Gamble.

The operative part of total quality is exceeding consumer expectations. Through our commitment to exceed their expectations, we hope that we will maintain and sustain competitive advantage.[5]

Based upon these and other perspectives on TQM, the following is a composite definition.

TQM is a top-down management philosophy focused on monitoring process variation, employee involvement, and continuous quality improvement in order to meet customer needs.

We will now look at each component of this definition in turn.

Top-Down Philosophy.   TQM efforts originate with top management and flow down the organization through goals identified in the strategic plan. Organizational change efforts generally only succeed when backed by the influence of top management.

Monitoring Process Variation.   TQM focuses on process variation rather than product variability. This is a major change in thinking for many managers who focus on problems with the product as their major concern. In TQM they must redirect their basic perspective toward thinking about how their business processes operate and how they can be improved.

Any business operation is composed of a number of processes, such as a subassembly procedure in manufacturing or the paper flow in approving customer credit. In TQM these processes are first defined and mapped out (flowcharts). Then process variability is monitored graphically and statistically (statistical process control [SPC]). Indications of abnormal variability (outside of control limits) are identified and causes explored. Common (system) causes (inadequate raw materials, machines in need of repair, procedures that can be streamlined, people in need of training) are identified and improved in order to reduce variability. Organizations have traditionally focused on managing performance through trying to manipulate special causes (rewarding or punishing individual employee performance from day to day).[6] TQM proposes that special causes have little effect (individuals can accomplish little by themselves independent from other influences in the organization); common causes should be managed instead.

Employee Involvement.   TQM uses employee teams to monitor process variability and generate quality improvement ideas. TQM is top-down, structured employee involvement, while other involvement efforts, such as quality circles, are bottom-up, unstructured efforts that have been largely unsuccessful.[7] Further, in TQM, teamwork, rather than individual effort, is the focus in performance evaluation and organizational rewards.

Employee teams monitor variability and generate quality improvement ideas through the Walter A. Shewhart plan, do, check, act (PDCA) cycle.

- Plan: Define the specific part of the process or problem to address.
- Do: Collect data about the baseline operation of the process.
- Check: Analyze the data to identify common causes that can be improved.
- Act: Implement suggested improvements.[8]

Continuous Quality Improvement. TQM revolves around continuous quality improvement. There are about as many definitions of quality as there are TQM experts. One definition that is fairly succinct yet at the same time comprehensive is "Quality is the degree to which customer needs and expectations are met with minimal variability in the product or service at a price that the customer will pay."[9] Customer needs and expectations can never be fully met. Further, customer demands change constantly. Thus, quality as total customer satisfaction is never met. The organization must try to improve quality continuously to remain competitive. Some examples of quality measures are errors in the process, customer satisfaction ratings, number of customer complaints, customer wait times for service, and accuracy of response to customers.

Theoretically, the emphasis on quality rather than traditional quantity productivity should result in higher profits. A quality emphasis focuses on doing the job right the first time, rather than reworking errors after the fact, which is extremely costly. Continuous quality improvement efforts also result in cost savings in operations. In addition, a reputation for having a quality product should increase market share.[10]

Customer Orientation. TQM focuses on the customer as the defining element in quality. TQM identifies two types of customer. *Internal customers* are those inside the organization (other departments that interact with a given unit, students for an academic department).

External customers are those outside of the organization (purchasers for a retail store, firms who hire a university's graduates).

LEADING VOICES IN THE QUALITY MOVEMENT

There are several leading voices in the quality movement.[11] Philip B. Crosby focuses on cost-integrated quality through conformance to requirements. He lists absolutes of quality management that include quality as conformance to requirements, quality is free (not doing the job right the first time costs money), the performance measurement is the expense of nonconformance, and the performance standard is zero defects. He proposes basic elements of improvement including the determination of top management to be serious about quality, education of everyone on the absolutes of quality management, and implementation of the quality process.[12]

J. M. Juran espouses company-wide quality integration flowing from hands-on leadership. He defines quality as fitness for use. He further specifies three major quality processes: quality planning (quality goals flowing from the strategic plan), quality control (measuring performance against quality standards), and quality improvement (working on extensive quality projects which leads to a breaking through toward unprecedented levels of performance).[13]

Kaoru Ishikawa looks to prevention of defects through customer orientation in his company-wide quality control: "The next process is your customer."[14] Genichi Taguchi defines quality as the loss a product causes to society through not meeting customer expectations, failure to meet performance characteristics, and harmful side effects. He focuses on design-integrated quality through analysis of multiple process variables.[15]

Deming's 14 Principles

Perhaps the name most associated with TQM is W. Edwards Deming who advocated both a radical change toward an organizational culture of quality and extensive SPC. Actually, Deming did not use the term *TQM* himself, but preferred the label of *continuous quality improvement.*

In this book we will focus on Deming's ideas. His 14 principles and seven deadly diseases provide the TQM perspective for examining motivation in chapter 3, performance evaluation in chapter 5, attribution theory in chapter 6, and emerging issues in chapter 7. A brief summary of his 14 principles follows.[16]

1. *Create constancy of purpose.* Management must possess a long-term commitment toward continuous quality improvement. This implies a strategic plan that states this commitment and backs it up by channeling necessary resources toward quality improvement.

2. *Adopt the new philosophy.* Management must transform the organization, starting at the top, toward continuous quality improvement. All employees must adopt the idea that mistakes are costly. At the same time, mistakes are not inevitable. Doing it right the first time should be the norm.

3. *Cease mass inspection.* The U.S. tradition of mass inspection goes back to Frederick Winslow Taylor's scientific management.[17] Inspection, however, implies that the production process is inherently flawed; mistakes *are* inevitable. Workers focus on quantity produced with the knowledge that quality control inspectors will identify mistakes at the end of the assembly line. In actuality, the rework of identified problems is costly. Quality comes from improvement of the process of making the product, not inspection of the product after it has been produced.

4. *End the practice of competitive bidding on price alone.* The lowest-price bidder usually has emphasized cost cutting, rather than quality, in order to offer the lowest price. Competitive bidding thus results in highly variable vendor materials. Instead the manufacturer, as the buyer of raw materials, should cultivate a long-term relationship with a few reliable suppliers who show that they emphasize quality by having a TQM program in place.

5. *Improve constantly and forever quality.* Quality must be built into the process. The process is then continuously monitored by statistical control techniques, so that a problem can be corrected as it occurs, not after the fact.

6. *Institute training.* Management must learn how the processes in the system operate in order to be able to change them. New workers must learn their job tasks thoroughly through extensive training.

7. *Institute leadership.* Management must lead by focusing on quality improvement, removing barriers to improvement, empowering workers so that they may improve processes, and managing the system, rather than closely supervising workers. Managers should look at themselves as coaches for the employees rather than as order givers.

8. *Drive out fear.* Workers are afraid that if they report problems or suggest changes they will lose their jobs. Management must drive out the sources of fear. They must cease ignoring or even punishing worker suggestions and focus instead on positive acceptance of change.

9. *Break down barriers.* Traditionally workers identify with their job specializations and distrust employees from other areas. The resulting distrust sets up competing goals with other units and misperceptions of workers from other departments. Cross-functional teams must be set up to break down barriers among departments and set up areas of cooperation.

10. *Eliminate slogans and quotas.* Management slogans, such as Zero Defects, are worthless because they give workers no direction on how to improve the situation.

11. *Eliminate numerical quotas.* Quotas focus upon producing quantity rather than improving quality in production.

12. *Remove barriers that rob people of pride of work.* Employees basically want to do a good job and are frustrated when barriers deny them pride in their work. Typical barriers are poor training, faulty machines, and poor-quality raw materials. In addition, pay-for-performance mechanisms focus employees on achieving individual pay raises, while at the same time such mechanisms divert employees from focusing on work quality.

13. *Encourage education and self-improvement.* Workers need extensive training and opportunities for self-improvement in TQM activities, teamwork, and statistical procedures in order to make effective suggestions for continuous improvement in quality.

14. *Take action.* The cross-functional teams plan a course of action, test the action by SPC methods, and make corrections (the PDCA cycle).

Deming's Seven Deadly Diseases

Deming also listed seven deadly diseases that he believed hinder an organization from successfully moving toward a culture of continuous quality improvement.[18]

1. *Lack of constancy of purpose.* The short-term orientation of U.S. business constantly shifts the emphasis of firms to the improvement fad of the moment. Customers, employees, and managers are in a state of confusion about what the firm is trying to change and where it is going.

2. *Emphasis on short-term profits.* Quarterly profit data drive U.S. business decision makers, who are held to a short time frame by their stakeholders (financiers, stockholders, and the community). Short-term profits can be increased by deferring the costs of maintenance and training, reducing research and development budgets, and shipping everything produced to the marketplace regardless of its quality. Eventually the firm earns a reputation for wide variations in quality. Moreover, such firms find themselves playing catch-up in chasing constantly changing customer demand.

3. *Merit rating and evaluation of individual performance.* One of the most controversial of Deming's ideas is that the U.S. emphasis on individual performance appraisal, merit pay, management by objectives (MBO), and pay for performance is bad because these devices emphasize individual gain at the expense of the goals of the firm. Individuals are rewarded for maintaining the system rather than trying to change it. The emphasis is on quantity produced rather than quality. Further, Deming believed that fair ratings are impossible because of supervisor biases, worker competition, and organizational politics. In this environment, short-term thinking proliferates and long-term planning suffers.

   Deming advocated that everyone in the group should be paid the same. Others advocate more of a middle ground. Individual workers should be evaluated on quality accomplishments and contribution to the team. Teams should be evaluated on quality improvements and teamwork. Managers should be evaluated on leadership of the quality effort and customer satisfaction.[19]

4. *Mobility of management.* U.S. industry encourages job-hopping among managers. Managers have learned to make a name for themselves with quick fixes and short-term results, which they use as stepping stones for job offers from other companies. With management constantly moving in and out of the organization, leadership is continuously in turmoil. Constancy of purpose is impossible.

5. *Running a company on visible figures alone.* Managers focus on visible figures, such as quantity of production, sales volume, cash flow, and employee work time. The important data for quality improvement (indicators of customer satisfaction) are not as easily obtainable and are thus not collected.

6. *Excessive medical costs.* The spiraling costs in the medical sector generate increased medical benefits costs to the organization, which siphons off funds that could be used to improve quality.

7. *Excessive liability costs.* The contingency fee system of U.S. lawyers generates too many product liability cases as well as worker compensation cases which result in exorbitant settlements that must be paid by the organization out of money that could be used to improve quality.

Deming and Reward and Recognition

Interestingly Deming did not directly address reward and recognition. Perhaps because of his science background, he did not feel it necessary to deal with all the nuances of the many motivational principles and theories available. In contrast, his friendly rival, Juran, does borrow from job enrichment theory and goal setting.[20]

The closest that Deming comes to a motivational approach is his principle of pride in work. In brief, he believed that workers will naturally have pride in their work (similar to the early American idea of pride in craftsmanship) if management would break down barriers separating workers from each other and encourage worker participation in the quality improvement effort. Perhaps because he has focused on the large areas of organizational culture change and statistical control of processes, Deming has had surprisingly little to say about the human side of motivation and the reward and recognition process. This presents an excellent opportunity for this book to examine the reward and recognition process and underlying motivational principles in the next several chapters.

THE BALDRIGE AWARD

We now look at the Malcolm Baldrige National Quality Award, the highest award in the United States that a TQM organization can achieve. In chapter 4 on organizational examples of successful reward and recognition systems we will describe the programs of several of the Baldrige Award winners. In chapter 7 we look at how formal awards like the Baldrige Award affect the reward and recognition process in an organization.

Named for Malcolm Baldrige, former secretary of commerce in the Reagan administration, the Baldrige Award is bestowed by the Commerce Department in order to recognize U.S. companies with a record of excellence in quality. Most important, many companies use the award criteria as standards for measuring their efforts toward improving quality, regardless of whether they are candidates for the award. We will briefly examine the seven criteria (the percentage weight of each criterion to the overall award judgment is in parentheses).[21]

1. *Leadership* (10 percent). Senior executives are visibly involved in quality-related activities both inside and outside of the organization. Quality values are written down. All levels of management are actively involved in quality activities.

2. *Information and analysis* (7 percent). There are specific quality measures. Data are collected on customer requirements, operating processes, and supplier quality. Benchmark data are collected on competitors for comparisons of quality practices.

3. *Strategic quality planning* (6 percent). Operational and strategic plans reflect quality goals and customer orientation.

4. *Human resource utilization* (15 percent). Human resource staffing plans reflect quality goals. Procedures allow for employee involvement and empowerment. There is extensive training on quality improvement efforts. Compensation plans reward quality efforts.

5. *Quality assurance and products and services* (14 percent). Product design reflects customer requirements. Operations involve continuous quality improvement. Processes are analyzed for

out-of-control problems. Extensive data are collected on process control, procedures, product performance, supplier quality, and technology change. Cooperative efforts (partnerships, training, incentives, certification) are pursued to improve supplier quality.

6. *Quality results* (18 percent). Steady and continuous improvements in quality are documented. The firm must be in the top 20 percent of its domestic and foreign industry in quality. The firm's suppliers show at least three years of quality improvement.

7. *Customer satisfaction* (30 percent). A variety of data measures current and future customer requirements. Customer evaluation techniques are continuously improved. A variety of data is collected on customer wait times, accuracy of response to customers, customer complaints, returns, warranty costs, and customer satisfaction. Data show an increase in market share during at least three years.

THE ORGANIZATIONAL STRUCTURE OF TQM

While Deming did not directly lay out the structure of the organization necessary to implement TQM, others have refined a hierarchy of teams required to improve quality. Although TQM focuses on employee input into quality improvement, many organizations have evolved a top-down, structured approach in which cross-functional management–employee teams operate at different levels. This is necessary because unless top management is fully committed to TQM and provides the overall guidance and resources, the effort will not succeed. (One of the major problems with quality circles is that they are bottom-up oriented. Many good ideas from the circles may not be implemented because of lack of top-management support.) Various companies have different names for the quality teams but they operate in very similar manners.[22]

Executive Steering Committee. The executive steering committee (ESC), the quality improvement team (QIT), or the quality council composed of top managers from various divisions sets the stage for TQM. These groups first focus the direction of TQM by constructing the strategic plan focused on customer orientation and continuous quality improvement. They then charter the permanent teams.

Quality Management Boards.   Several quality management boards (QMBs) or quality teams composed of middle managers and worker leaders are responsible for monitoring major processes within the organization. The QMBs may identify certain problems and charter temporary teams to resolve the problems. Several companies have acknowledged that reward and recognition is a major process in the organization and have assigned full-time committees to monitor this process.

Process Action Teams.   The process action teams (PATs) or corrective action teams (CATs) are temporary committees set up by the QMBs to resolve specific problems. They are composed of representatives (including internal and sometimes external customers) from various departments who are directly involved with the part of the process in which the problem is embedded. They brainstorm causes of the problem, construct cause-and-effect diagrams and flowcharts of the process involved with the problem, collect data on various causes of the problem, and suggest improvements to resolve the problem. They are designed to be temporary teams and dissolve when the problem solution is implemented. They may have a formal ceremony, such as a dinner, in which they recognize their own efforts and then formally disband.

BOOK PREVIEW

Now that the basic TQM concepts have been defined, the stage is set to examine the reward and recognition process in more depth. This book divides this examination into three parts.

Part I examines characteristics of the reward and recognition process. Chapter 2 looks at principles of reward and recognition in TQM. Chapter 3 lays out motivational bases of reward and recognition as found in reinforcement theory, expectancy theory, goal-setting theory, and the job characteristics model. Chapter 4 presents organizational examples of reward and recognition efforts in the manufacturing, service, public, and international sectors. Chapter 5 presents the unique problems of performance evaluation under a TQM effort.

Part II examines special issues in reward and recognition. Chapter 6 discusses an attribution theory approach to understanding supervisor and worker behavior under TQM, which has implications for the reward and recognition process. Chapter 7 presents three emerging issues in reward and recognition that must be confronted if TQM is to remain viable into the future: the role of charismatic leadership, the role of competition, and the role of formal state and national quality awards. In addition, the impact of work force diversity on TQM is discussed.

Part III concludes the material. Chapter 8 ties together the material from the previous chapters through means for continuous improvement of the reward and recognition process. Chapter 9 looks at what we already know about reward and recognition and what we still need to know.

NOTES

1. A good summary of the ideas of the quality leaders is in Robert R. Gehani, "Quality Value Chain: A Meta-Synthesis of Frontiers of the Quality Movement," *Academy of Management Executive* 7 (spring 1993): 29–42.

2. Marshall Sashkin and Kenneth J. Kiser, *Total Quality Management* (Seabrook, Md.: Ducochon Press, 1991), 25.

3. Richard D. Spitzer, "TQM in Commercial Banking" (paper presented at the Louisiana Quality Symposium, Baton Rouge, La., October 1991).

4. Laura L. Matherly and H. Alan Lasater, "Implementing TQM in a Hospital," *Quality Progress* 25 (April 1992): 81–88.

5. Karen Bemowski, "Carrying on the P & G Tradition," *Quality Progress* 25 (May 1992): 21–26.

6. W. Edwards Deming, *Out of the Crisis* (Cambridge, Mass.: MIT Center for Advanced Engineering Study, 1986), 314.

7. Michael White and Paula Konoske, *An Evaluation of Quality Circles in Department of Defense Organizations*, NPRDC-89-9 (San Diego, Calif.: Navy Personnel Research and Development Center, 1989).

8. Deming, *Out of the Crisis*, 88.

9. Delbert Nebeker and Michael White, "Team-Oriented Performance Management," concept paper (San Diego, Calif.: Navy Personnel Research and Development Center, 1990), 3.

10. Deming, *Out of the Crisis*, 3.

11. The ideas of the quality leaders are summarized in Gehani, "Quality Value Chain," and presented in more depth in James R. Evans and William M. Lindsay, *The Management and Control of Quality*, 2d ed. (Minneapolis: West, 1993).

12. Philip B. Crosby, *Quality Is Free* (New York: McGraw-Hill, 1979).

13. J. M. Juran, *Juran on Leadership for Quality* (New York: Free Press, 1989).

14. Kaoru Ishikawa and David J. Lu, *What is Total Quality Control? The Japanese Way* (Englewood Cliffs, N.J.: Prentice Hall, 1985).

15. Genichi Taguchi, *Introduction to Quality Engineering* (Tokyo: Asian Productivity Organization, 1986).

16. Besides Deming's *Out of the Crisis*, very readable descriptions of his 14 principles occur in Mary Walton's two books, *The Deming Management Method* (New York: Putnam, 1986) and *Deming Management at Work* (New York: Putnam, 1990).

17. Stephen B. Knouse, Paula Phillips Carson, and Kerry D. Carson, "W. Edwards Deming and Frederick Winslow Taylor: A Comparison of Two Leaders Who Shaped the World's View of Management," *International Journal of Public Administration* 16 (October 1993): 1621–58.

18. Deming, *Out of the Crisis;* Walton, *The Deming Management Method;* Walton, *Deming Management at Work.*

19. Jim M. Graber, Roger E. Breisch, and Walter E. Breisch, "Performance Appraisals and Deming: A Misunderstanding?" *Quality Progress* 25 (June 1992): 59–62; Barry R. Nathan, John Milliman, and Nida Backaitis, "The Deming Challenge to Performance Appraisal: Implications for Research and Practice" (paper presented at the annual meeting of the Society of Industrial and Organizational Psychologists, St. Louis, Mo., April 1991).

20. Juran, *Juran on Leadership for Quality.*

21. A good summary of the Baldrige Award criteria is in M. G. Brown, "Measuring Your Company against the Baldrige Criteria," *Journal of Quality and Participation* 13 (June 1991): 82–88.

22. A detailed description of TQM team structure is in Archester Houston and Steven Dockstader, *A Total Quality Management Process Improvement Model*, NPRDC-TR-89-3 (San Diego, Calif., Navy Personnel Research and Development Center, 1988).

Part I

The Reward and Recognition Process

Chapter 2

Principles of the Reward and Recognition Process

Genuine recognition of performance is something people really appreciate.

People really don't work for money. They go to work for it, but once the salary has been established, their concern is appreciation. Recognize their contribution publicly and noisily, but don't demean them by applying a price tag to everything.
—Philip B. Crosby, *Quality Is Free*

While most managers agree that reward and recognition are important, this process is many times one of the last to be formally designed and integrated into the TQM effort. Why do managers leave such an important process for last? Perhaps they are taking a cue from Deming that the only real motivator is pride in work, which is intrinsic to the worker and his or her work.[1] Perhaps they believe that the reward and recognition system is already in place and simply needs fine-tuning. They see other more vital problems as coming first. The upshot, however, is that many times the reward and recognition process is not being managed well. Consequently, rewards, awards, and other indicators of recognition may be ineffective—not appreciated or even desired by employees and manipulated by managers for their own purposes.

In order to understand this process, we will first look at what constitutes reward, its functions, and principles for its use. Then we will look at pay as a reward system. Next we will look at recognition—what it is, its functions, and principles for its use. Finally we will examine a hypothetical example of how a reward and recognition quality team might manage the reward and recognition process in a TQM organization.

17

REWARD

Psychologists define *reward* somewhat differently depending upon their perspective. A behaviorist defines reward as anything that increases the frequency of behavior.[2] This is an operational definition. Reward is defined in terms of how it operates on behavior. The important point is that the reward dispenser (here a manager) must give out rewards that work—that actually improve employee behavior. The key is that there are differences in employee reactions to various rewards. One employee may react well to praise. Another may work hard to receive a covered parking place. Many employees, but not all, will work hard to receive a bonus. Still other employees will work hard at creating suggestions for improving quality, if they are allowed to present their ideas to a receptive audience.

Some psychologists argue that tangible rewards, such as money or objects earned, may actually reduce intrinsic motivation—doing something for its own sake.[3] In the TQM organization they would argue that rewards, such as bonuses, might destroy intrinsic motivation, such as doing the job for its own satisfaction—what Deming would call pride in work. Managers have little to fear, however. There are literally thousands of studies that show that reward is effective in changing behavior. If reward works, then, it makes sense to manage reward in the reward and recognition process, rather than let it occur arbitrarily.

Functions of Reward

What are the various functions of reward in the TQM organization?

- *Improve TQM Behaviors.* A managed reward system focuses on improving desired behaviors. In the case of the TQM organization, reward can improve TQM behaviors—working in teams, using TQM tools, solving quality problems, interacting with both internal and external customers.

- *Improve TQM Culture.* Corporate culture has several essential components—corporate values, leadership, and the reward structure of the organization.[4] The reward system reflects the corporate philosophy—democratic and innovative or autocratic and stifling. Further, reward cements employee commitment to corporate values in the corporate culture. Indeed, reward serves to internalize organization values, such as quality, in the employees.[5]

Many believe that TQM is actually a change in corporate culture to an environment of continuous quality improvement. Reward then serves to reinforce the commitment to quality improvement in the organization. In Deming's terms, reward can help transform the organization toward a philosophy of quality.[6]

- *Visible Statement of Organizational Values.* The reward system makes a statement about what is important to the organization. It is a public statement about the priorities of the organization—quality, customer satisfaction, and continuous improvement.[7]

Principles for an Effective Reward System

There are several principles for setting up an effective reward system in an organization.[8]

- *The Reward Is Valued.* Employees must have a preference for the types of rewards being offered. Many employees prefer cash awards and plaques. Some employees like to see their name in the company newsletter. Others like the public recognition surrounding award ceremonies.

- *The System Is Simple to Understand.* Elaborate procedures for evaluating performance, filling out forms, and review by several levels of management lead to confusion. The system must be easy to understand if it is to be used effectively.

- *Performance Standards Are Within the Control of the Team.* Performance standards must be realistic—challenging yet attainable. With hard work the team members should be able to reach the standards.

- *Supervisors Are Motivated to Maintain the System.* Supervisors have the power to make the system work or manipulate it for personal purposes. If supervisors, however, view the reward system as basically fair and effective, most will work to maintain it.

- *Employees Have Input into Installing the System.* Employee participation in the process and empowerment to change the process are major components of an effective TQM program.

Besides, who knows better than employees what rewards are effective for them?

- *There Is Open Communication.* If organizations practice open communication (as opposed to secrecy), employees are encouraged to share ideas and information. In an open system, where all procedures and consequences are visible, administration of the reward system has to be efficient, fair, and equitable; employees see the results. A secret system breeds rumors, false beliefs, and misperceptions about who has received rewards and about the rewards they received.

Types of Reward

There are four basic types of reward available to the TQM organization. Table 2.1 summarizes the following section.

1. *Cash.* Although employees have individual preferences for rewards, most react favorably to cash. In fact, money is considered to be a generalized reward that will work almost anywhere with almost anyone. Cash rewards can be in the form of bonuses or raises.

2. *Gain sharing versus profit sharing.* A number of TQM companies reward their employees with a percentage of the share of the cost savings or profits from TQM efforts. It is important here to distinguish such sharing as gain sharing or profit sharing.

TABLE 2.1.   Types of reward and recognition.

Level	Financial	Awards	Other Recognitions
Individual	Bonus	Excellence	Trips
	Profit sharing	Initiative	Desk items
	Gain sharing	Effort	Pins and jewelry
	Skill-based pay	Team	News articles
		Contribution	Pictures prominently displayed
Team	Bonus	Excellence	News articles
	Gain sharing	Initiative	Family outings
	Group pay	Effort	Team presentations
		Teamwork	Conference trips
			Items with team logo

Gain sharing is more focused on specific TQM teams that make improvement suggestions and then are allowed a percentage of the resulting cost savings. All teams do not participate. Profit sharing, on the other hand, is more general. The company gives percentage shares of profits to all individuals or teams equally.[9]

3. *Nonmonetary rewards.* There are three types of nonmonetary rewards: symbols, things people use, and other forms of recognition.[10] Symbols include praise from supervisors and co-workers; badges (for example, decals and signs) that denote accomplishments; and public accolades from the organization, like formal presentations of awards and formal dinners. Things people use include tokens, such as pens, calculators, pins, and other jewelry. These things may also incorporate symbols of the TQM effort, like TQM or team logos.

4. *Team rewards.* Judith Mower, a human resources expert, suggests that team rewards (where all team members receive rewards) produce the best team performance. She suggests that rewards that support rather than detract from intrinsic motivation should be considered, rewards should be given throughout a project's life, and the most effective reward is one that the team invents for itself.[11]

Team rewards are generally implemented when TQM has become firmly implanted in the organization. At this point teams are functioning well in problem solving and continuous process improvement. During TQM implementation, the organizational reward structure may progress through many phases: first traditional pay for performance, like merit pay; then individual and key contributor incentives; then gain sharing and skill-based pay; and finally team rewards.[12]

PAY AS REWARD

Any discussion of reward systems inevitably leads to examining the role of pay in the organization. Even Taylor, the father of scientific management (which many believe is the antithesis of TQM), believed that if you increased a worker's productivity, you should increase his or her pay accordingly.[13]

Deming and Traditional Pay Systems

Deming was against any type of pay system that promotes the individual over the organization.[14] Most of our traditional types of pay, such as merit pay and commission, depend on the individual competing against others for a scarce pool of money for raises. The individual must necessarily play a zero sum game where he or she tries to maximize his or her own gain at the expense of the pay raises of others. Individual competition flourishes and any type of teamwork or cooperation falls by the wayside.

Some see Deming as advocating that all employees should be paid the same, which would reinforce an organization-wide approach to pay. The problem is that our culture strongly emphasizes pay as reward for performance.[15] Any pay system then that supports TQM must emphasize some type of performance relationship. There are a number of innovative pay ideas floating around that support TQM in various ways.

Pay as Sharing in Cost Savings

Profit Sharing. Profit sharing has been around for some time, going back at least to the Scanlon Plan, where employee suggestions were turned into cash based on the cost reductions that accrued. The basic form of profit sharing takes a share of the company's profits for a year and divides them equally among the employees. Deming's idea of equal pay is thus emphasized. Furthermore, profit sharing follows logically from Deming's view that quality improvement should result in profitability, because expensive rework is reduced, quality improvements lead to cost efficiencies, and a reputation for quality will increase market share for the company.[16] Inevitably, the company makes a profit from TQM. Thus the employees should share equally in that profit.

The problem, however, is that profitability can also be attained by laying off skilled workers, cutting research and development costs, and cutting training costs. All of these actions, of course, are detrimental to TQM.

Gain Sharing. Gain sharing is generally more focused than profit sharing. Employee teams make improvement suggestions, which result in a cost savings when implemented. The team then shares part of the cost savings. Unless they were directly involved in the improvement, other teams in the organization do not share in this particular effort (they may share in others that they instigate).

The advantage of gain sharing over profit sharing is that it focuses on producing cost efficiencies and cost savings from quality improvements, rather than emphasizing any means that would produce a profit. For example, at Evart Products, an automobile parts firm, gain sharing reduced the defective products rate, increased supplier quality assurance survey scores, and helped Evart win several quality awards from their customers like Chrysler and Volkswagen.[17] The problem with gain sharing, however, is that it may produce a competition among teams for maximizing their own cost-saving ideas, which would reduce cooperation among teams necessary for the TQM effort.

Pay Based on Skill Acquisition

Skill-based pay, or paying for employee skill development rather than employee productivity, would fit nicely within a TQM framework. Indeed, a number of high employee involvement organizations, including TQM organizations, use some variation of skill-based pay.[18] Because two of Deming's 14 principles emphasize education and training, TQM organizations already invest large sums into employees acquiring and maintaining TQM skills, such as statistical tools, teamwork, and problem solving. It is therefore logical that, because they value these skills, organizations should pay their employees to acquire these skills both on and off the job. Moreover, skill-based pay reinforces the importance of TQM skill development in the organizational culture. Skill-based pay would reward employees for acquiring a variety of abilities, which improves cooperation and teamwork, and would enhance the flexibility of the organization in identifying and implementing new ideas for quality improvement.

One example of a successful merger of quality improvement and skill-based pay involves a Midwestern manufacturing firm. It allowed production teams to develop their own skill-based pay system where team members could move through five pay levels based on peer evaluation. Skill acquisition was anchored to meeting quality standards set by the teams' customers.[19]

Pay for Team-Oriented Performance

TQM also emphasizes teamwork and cooperation. Therefore, an effective pay system could reward team-based performance.

Contribution Increases. A few organizations are experimenting with pay raises given for team contributions. TQM teams and supervisors rate individuals on their contributions to the team effort, which is then translated into their pay raise. In at least one company, everyone in the group receives the same raise, which satisfies Deming's pay equality principle.[20]

Group Variable Pay. Other companies are experimenting with pay raises given for meeting or exceeding goals on collaborative performance. In some companies this becomes a bonus and, thus, is not included in base pay. The implication is that the bonus may increase or decrease depending on performance toward goals. This follows from the TQM concept that continuous improvement means change.[21] Such programs are closer to the Japanese concept that a large part of the total compensation package is composed of bonuses rather than base pay. Thus the pay of Japanese can fluctuate greatly from year to year.

Group variable pay focuses on performance toward group goals of quality improvement. Some TQM goals that companies pursue are[22]

- *Retention of customers.* The customer defines quality according to TQM. TQM requires close relationships with customers to design products and services to meet customer needs. Thus retention of these valued customers is important.

- *External customer satisfaction.* TQM organizations strive to satisfy their customers in the marketplace better than their competitors. They solve customer problems rather than hide them.

- *Internal customer satisfaction.* Deming advocated breaking down barriers between departments and employee groups.[23] Serving rather than hindering demands for information, resources, and assistance allows better servicing of the key processes of the organization and also builds an atmosphere of trust and cooperation needed for TQM.

- *Product and service reliability.* TQM procedures reduce variability in organizational processes. The resulting products and services are of consistently high quality.

Criteria for Effective TQM Pay Systems

There is no one best way to develop an effective pay system that supports TQM. Indeed, the TQM concept of continuous improvement implies that the pay system is undergoing continuing monitoring and change in order to make it constantly better. There are a number of criteria, however, that should be met in any effective TQM pay system.

- *Effective communications.* Research on collective pay-for-performance systems shows that strong communication is vital.[24] TQM pay plans by their very nature tend to be complex and different from what employees traditionally expect. Open and extensive communication of the procedures and the reasons for the plan are important.

- *Employee involvement.* The collective pay research also shows that a high level of employee involvement is necessary.[25] Managers must allow employees active participation in selecting and implementing these new and different plans. Theoretically, employees should be motivated by participating in pay plan development for two reasons. First they understand the plan better. Second they acquire a sense of ownership of the plan because it was in part derived from their ideas. Process ownership is, of course, a major factor in successful TQM organizations.[26]

- *Win–win pay philosophy.* Any pay system that is based on a zero sum game that pits employees or teams against one another to maximize their own gain at the expense of others in the organization will magnify internal competition and reduce cooperation. Any type of bonus program for a cost-savings or improvement suggestion must be available to all, creating a win–win perspective on pay.[27] Management must continuously monitor this type of program to ensure that bonuses are not concentrated in only a few hands.

  Bonus plans assume profitability. What happens when the company inevitably faces a financial downturn and reduced profitability? This is many times a function of the overall economy and not the TQM efforts of a given company. One alternative is not to give all bonuses immediately, but to allow employee team members to defer part of their bonus for "hard times." This would also emphasize long-term profitability and get away from Deming's deadly disease of a myopic view toward immediate profits.[28]

- *Process improvement.* It is easy to slip into another of Deming's deadly diseases—focusing on easy numbers—paying employees to meet productivity and sales quotas.[29] Instead, the pay system should be geared to improving the process of producing the product or service. Goals should focus on procedures and uses of resources that minimize process variability and maximize customer satisfaction.

- *Employee stake in the organization.* Some advocates of TQM believe that the primary ingredient to successful TQM is giving employees a significant stake in the organization.[30] Employees will become more seriously involved when they are suggesting improvement to their own organization. Perhaps this is the ultimate form of ownership of the processes; the employees literally own a part of the company.

  Employee stakeholding has implications for the areas of profit sharing as well as compensation packaging. Management might consider sharing with employees the profits from TQM efforts through employee stock purchasing programs.[31] Or, profits could be shared through some type of cafeteria compensation plan, where employees would have a choice in allocating their share toward pensions or insurance benefits.

RECOGNITION

Recognition, the public acknowledgment of successes, also can be highly motivating if managed correctly. Recognition serves various functions, including the following.

Functions of Recognition

- *Indicator of achievement.* Some forms of recognition, such as awards and plaques, show publicly that the individual or team has achieved some degree of success with TQM. They are a visible indicator both to the team and to outsiders of a job well-done.
- *Feedback.* Recognition is also a form of feedback about the results of individual or team efforts. It shows the individuals or the teams that they are on the right track toward continuous improvement. Recognition as feedback can come from supervisors, other teams, internal customers in the organization, or external customers in the marketplace.

- *Show the organization's appreciation for effort.* Recognition highlights employees and teams who make a definite contribution to the TQM effort. Such recognition stimulates further effort in employees.

Principles for Recognition Systems

Several principles underlie the effective use of recognition.[32]

- *Recognition should be immediate.* Recognition should be timely and relate to specific accomplishments. The award or plaque should be given as close to the accomplishment as possible. The presentation ceremony should reinforce how the recognition specifically relates to the accomplishment.

- *Recognition should be personal.* Recognition is a direct contact between employees and managers; it is a joint celebration of accomplishments improving the organization. To ensure a personal touch, employees should participate in determining the forms of recognition.

- *Recognition is not compensation.* Compensation is long-term and fairly inflexible once it is set (it is almost impossible to reduce pay levels once set). Employees come to expect raises. Recognition, on the other hand, is immediate and flexible. Recognition ceremonies can occur at any time. Forms of recognition (for example, types of awards) can constantly change to suit changing employee preferences and new types of TQM efforts.

- *Employees should believe recognition is not based on luck.* If employees believe that recognition is controlled by events beyond their control, they will reduce their efforts (why try if recognition occurs whether you try or not?). Eventually, employees will become cynical about the recognition system. Instead employees should believe that recognition is a direct organizational response to their efforts toward continuous improvement.

- *Recognition systems should not create winners and losers.* Recognition should not be a zero sum game where for one individual or team to win recognition someone else must forego recognition. The same individuals or teams should not be recognized continually to the detriment of others. Rather, diverse types of recognition (for example, awards, signs, plaques, presentations, and articles in company publications) should be available to all.

- *Recognition should be given for efforts, not just attainments.* Attainments are readily measured while efforts leading to attainments—such as trying out new techniques to improve customer satisfaction and suggesting improvements to procedures that may be difficult to implement immediately—may be harder to measure. It is important to recognize good efforts as well as end results.

- *Employees should participate in recognition programs.* Employee participation is important to ensure that management is recognizing what employees think is important. Further, employee participation ensures the perception that the recognition system is fair.

Types of Recognition

There are several types of recognition that an organization can offer. The important point is that the company has a number of recognition options available that it can build on to ensure immediate, fair, personalized, and innovative recognition.

Company Awards.   The most common form of recognition in TQM programs is some type of company quality award to individuals or teams: President's Award, Excellence in Quality Award, Team Excellence Award, Idea Development Award, Contribution Award, Initiative Award, and Exceptional Effort Award. This type of award is usually in the form of a plaque or certificate presented at a formal recognition meeting (see Table 2.1).

Continuous quality improvement requires innovation, and innovation should occur in the recognition process as with any other important process. Innovative variations on individual awards are company-financed trips, pins and other jewelry with TQM logos, parking spaces, articles in company newsletters, and employees' pictures on the bulletin boards or entrances to the building.[33]

Innovative variations on team awards include articles in company newsletters, family recognition picnics, team progress presentations to upper management or customers, company-financed team attendance at quality conferences, and team mementos (pens, calculators, or product models with team TQM logos).[34]

Team-Managed Awards. Several TQM companies offer quality awards that are managed by teams. Teams nominate other teams. In some companies the team even creates a customized award for the winning team. Management provides the cash with which the nominating team then buys something or makes something that uniquely characterizes the winning team—a sign or tokens such as mugs, badges, or T-shirts with the team name or logo.

Customer Awards. Because TQM focuses on meeting customer expectations, it makes sense that customer satisfaction should translate into awards to individuals and teams for particularly good work for the customer. In many companies customers are part of the award nomination and presentation process.[35]

THE OPERATION OF A HYPOTHETICAL REWARD AND RECOGNITION PROCESS

Reward and recognition is an important process in the organizational TQM effort. Therefore, it must be monitored and managed through the organizational TQM structure as any other important process. The following is an illustration of the steps that a typical reward and recognition team in a TQM organization might follow in managing the reward and recognition process.

Team Charter.   The team is chartered as a permanent quality team by the TQM Executive Steering Committee (ESC) composed of top managers, customers, and worker leaders.

Team Mission.   The ESC sets the mission to be continuous improvement of the reward and recognition process. The budget for awards is $50,000.[36]

Team Philosophy.   The reward and recognition team decides to adopt as its philosophy a common phrase used by many TQM quality teams, "Just do it!"

Team Composition.   Team members include a human resources manager, a representative of the union local, an employee representative from each department of the company, a representative from the company's largest external customer, and the TQM facilitator (an employee who has gone through extensive TQM training and who assists the team in using TQM tools). The team leader is elected by the team.

Team Functions

1. *Monitor the reward and recognition process.* The team composes an elaborate diagram of how the various rewards and awards in the company flow: the nomination procedure, evaluation procedures, paperwork, review levels, and the operation of recognition ceremonies.

2. *Identify problem areas.* Based upon its diagram and continuing surveying of employees, managers, and customers, the team identifies problematic areas in the reward and recognition process.

3. *Create Process Action Teams (PATs) to solve problems.* The team charters temporary PATs to resolve an identified problem. When the problem is resolved and solution implemented, the PAT is dissolved.

After one year the reward and recognition team identifies the following problem areas.

- Reward and recognition are given too often for quantity rather than quality produced.
- Too many individual awards are given, too few team awards exist.
- Performance evaluation systems focus on individual accomplishments rather than team efforts in TQM.
- There is a lack of motivating nonmonetary awards.

The reward and recognition team temporarily charters a nonmonetary award PAT to address the problem of the lack of motivating nonmonetary awards. The team is composed of two members of the reward and recognition team (to ensure that the PAT keeps on target), three worker representatives, two managers, an external customer representative, and a TQM facilitator drawn from a pool of experienced facilitators that the company maintains. The PAT formulates the following action plan to resolve the problem of nonmonetary awards.

1. *Diagram existing awards process.* The PAT takes the master reward and recognition diagram and extends it for the awards process.

2. *Survey stakeholders.* The team formulates an award survey that identifies motivational and administrative problems in awards

and asks for suggestions for new types of awards. The survey is administered to managers, employees, and external customers.

3. *Set up a prototype award.* Based on the survey results, the PAT concludes that customized awards and team awards would be motivating and that quality teams should be involved in the award process. The PAT then creates a prototype award where quality teams nominate other teams. The company provides the money to buy the award. The nominating team then uses the money to create a customized award that fits with the style and personality of the nominated team.

4. *Run a test of the prototype.* The PAT decides to run a test of the prototype on three departments in the company for six months.

5. *Refine and implement award system.* The PAT refines some minor problems (nomination procedures) and suggests implementation to the reward and recognition team, which implements the Team Nomination Award company-wide.

6. *PAT has its own recognition ceremony and disbands.* As its final action, the PAT has a dinner for its members, financed by the ESC, where it recognizes its achievement and formally disbands.

CONCLUSIONS

We have examined a number of principles of reward and recognition as well as variations on types of reward and recognition that organizations can confer on individuals and teams. We have also looked at how a hypothetical reward and recognition team might run the reward and recognition process. One point that should be emphasized is diversity. There is a diversity of preferences for reward and recognition among the different kinds of individuals and teams in the organization, and there is a diversity of types of reward, pay, and recognition available that the organization can implement. Therefore, the reward and recognition team should create a wide variety of well-publicized rewards and awards. Such an environment will not only address individual and team differences in preferences, but will create a win–win situation where many different types of improvement efforts and quality accomplishment can be rewarded.

NOTES

1. W. Edwards Deming, *Out of the Crisis* (Cambridge, Mass.: MIT Center for Advanced Engineering Study, 1986), 77.

2. The most prominent behaviorist was B. F. Skinner who laid out the principles of behaviorism in his book *Contingencies of Reinforcement* (New York: Appleton-Century-Crofts, 1969).

3. Edward L. Deci, "The Effect of Externally Mediated Rewards on Intrinsic Motivation," *Journal of Personality and Social Psychology* (1971): 105–15.

4. A current examination of corporate culture is in Harrison M. Trice and Janice M. Beyer, *The Cultures of Work Organizations* (Englewood Cliffs, N.J.: Prentice Hall, 1993).

5. Helga Drummond and Elizabeth Chell, "Should Organizations Pay for Quality?" *Personnel Review* 21, no. 4 (1992): 3–11.

6. Deming, *Out of the Crisis,* 26.

7. Brooks Carder and James D. Clark, "The Theory and Practice of Employee Recognition," *Quality Progress* 25 (December 1992): 25–30.

8. Edward E. Lawler, "The Design of Effective Reward Systems," in *Handbook of Organizational Behavior,* ed. J. W. Lorsch (Englewood Cliffs, N.J.: Prentice Hall, 1987), 255–71; B. P. Pelletier and M. A. Rahim, "Total Quality Management and Drawbacks of Incentive Systems," *Industrial Management* 35 (January 1993): 4–6.

9. Marshall Sashkin and Kenneth J. Kiser, *Total Quality Management* (Seabrook, Md.: Ducochon Press, 1991).

10. Virginia Johnson, "Total Quality Management," *Successful Meetings* 41 (June 1992): 100–103.

11. John G. Johnson, "Rewarding the Right Behaviors," *Tapping the Network Journal* 3 (March 1992): 21–24.

12. Sam T. Johnson, "Work Teams: What's Ahead in Work Design and Rewards Management," *Compensation and Benefits Review* 25 (March–April 1993): 35–41.

13. Stephen B. Knouse, Paula Phillips Carson, and Kerry D. Carson, "W. Edwards Deming and Frederick Winslow Taylor: A Comparison of Two Leaders Who Shaped the World's View of Management," *International Journal of Public Administration* 16 (October 1993): 1621–58.

14. Deming, *Out of the Crisis,* 102.

15. David E. Bowen and Edward E. Lawler, "Total Quality-Oriented Human Resources Management," *Organizational Dynamics* (spring 1992): 29–41.

16. Deming, *Out of the Crisis,* 3.

17. Timothy L. Ross and Larry Hatcher, "Gainsharing Drives Quality Improvement," *Personnel Journal* (November 1992): 81–89.

18. Edward E. Lawler, Gerald E. Ledford, and Lei Chang, "Who Uses Skill-Based Pay, and Why," *Compensation and Benefits Review* 25 (March–April 1993): 22–26.

19. Arthur G. Dobbelaere and Kathleen H. Goeppinger, "The Right Way and the Wrong Way to Set up a Self-Directed Work Team," *Human Resources Professional* 5 (Winter 1993): 31–35.

20. David Burda, "Hospital Employs TQM Principles to Rework its Evaluation System," *Modern Healthcare* 22 (August 1992): 60.

21. Patricia L. Zingheim and Jay R. Schuster, "Linking Quality and Pay," *HRMagazine* (December 1992): 55–59.

22. Ibid.

23. Deming, *Out of the Crisis,* 77.

24. Bowen and Lawler, "Total Quality-Oriented Human Resources Management."

25. Ibid.

26. Edwin A. Locke and David M. Schweiger, "Participation in Decision Making," in *Research in Organizational Behavior,* vol. 1, ed. Barry M. Staw (Greenwich, Conn.: JAI Press, 1978).

27. Zingheim and Schuster, "Linking Quality and Pay."

28. Deming, *Out of the Crisis,* 99.

29. Ibid.

30. Drummond and Chell, "Should Organizations Pay for Quality?"

31. Bowen and Lawler, "Total Quality-Oriented Human Resources Management."

32. Carder and Clark, "The Theory and Practice of Employee Recognition."

33. Descriptions of types of recognition possible are in H. James Harrington, *The Improvement Process* (New York: McGraw-Hill, 1987); Kathryn Troy, "Recognize Quality Achievement with Noncash Awards," *Personnel Journal* (October 1993): 111–17.

34. Ibid.

35. A recent survey of TQM companies reported by Kathryn Troy (note 33) showed that 53 percent of service firms involved customers in award nominations, while only 20 percent of durable goods manufacturers involved customers.

36. The Troy survey (note 33) showed an overall median budget of $50,000 for awards, while manufacturers report a median budget of $37,000 and service firms report a median budget of $80,000.

Chapter 3

Motivational Bases of Reward and Recognition

Motivation is part of every human exchange
—Philip B. Crosby, Quality Is Free

Human needs are extensive, perhaps limitless
—J. M. Juran, Managerial Breakthrough

One of the central issues—if not the central issue—in consider-
ing motivation in work situations concerns the reward system
utilized in and by the organization.
—Richard M. Steers and Lyman W. Porter,
Motivation and Work Behavior

Motivation is a primary factor in human behavior. The basic definition of *motivation* is that which initiates, directs, and maintains behavior.[1] Motivation theorists make an analogy to a car battery. Like the battery starting the car, motivation starts behavior. Then motivation directs behavior toward a certain goal and keeps the behavior going until the goal is reached.

There are several prominent theories of motivation in the organizational behavior literature whose effectiveness has been demonstrated by extensive research. Surprisingly, the quality management literature contains very little about how to integrate these motivational theories into TQM practice. This chapter attempts to begin to rectify this neglect. Several well-established theories of motivation are discussed. From each theory important principles of motivation are derived that may improve the reward and recognition process. Examples of how TQM organizations apply these principles occur in chapter 4.

REINFORCEMENT THEORY

Reinforcement theory as presented by the behaviorists has been termed an environmental theory because it states that behavior is controlled by the environment surrounding behavior.[2] Specifically, events immediately preceding behavior (antecedents) and events immediately following behavior (consequences) control behavior (see Figure 3.1).

Consequences are the important factor here. Negative consequences, such as punishment, decrease behavior, which is effective for controlling undesirable behavior. Although punishment can be effective for reducing undesirable behavior, it has negative side effects, such as anger and fear. Most psychologists prefer to use punishment only as a last resort. Most TQM managers would agree. Deming desired to drive out fear, not create it.

Positive consequences, such as reinforcement, increase desirable behavior. Obviously, this is the consequence that TQM managers are interested in.

Antecedents ⟶ Behavior ⟶ Consequences

FIGURE 3.1.   Behavioral model.

Reinforcement

The definition of *reinforcement* follows the behavioristic definition of *reward* given in chapter 2—anything that increases behavior. This definition allows for a lot of flexibility. TQM managers could potentially use a large number of reinforcers.

- Money
- Office enhancers (a bigger desk, a window, pictures for the wall)
- Prime parking spaces
- Increased responsibilities
- Social reinforcers (praise, attention, the chance to present TQM successes to others)

The important point is that TQM managers must focus on things that work—that actually improve behavior. They have to pay attention to individual differences in preferences among employees and quality teams.

In reinforcement theory this is termed *prior reinforcement history.* Each individual or team has a set of reward preferences based upon his or her prior experience with types of rewards.

Unfortunately, reinforcement also can have a negative side. Negative reinforcement is the situation where the individual works hard to avoid a negative consequence from occurring. For example, employees will work hard to avoid being yelled at or humiliated by supervisors or peers. Just as with punishment (which decreases behavior) negative reinforcement (which increases behavior) has the undesirable side effects of anger and fear. Therefore, TQM managers must avoid using negative reinforcement (threats of negative consequences) to control behavior, if they are to drive out fear.

Contingent Reinforcement

One of the primary principles of managing reinforcers is contingency. Effective reinforcers must be given immediately after the desired behavior and be associated with the desired behavior by the individual. Praise is effective because it is generally given right after an employee does something well, and the employee can associate praise with good work.

Many reinforcers in the workplace are ineffective because they are noncontingent on the behavior they are supposed to be improving. Year-end annual raises and bonuses are intended to be rewarding but usually occur months after the behavior they are supposed to enhance. Consequently, they become looked upon as an employee right rather than a reward for good work.

Organizational Behavior Modification

There are a large number of studies that show that reinforcement theory is effective in improving organizational behaviors, such as absenteeism, productivity, safety behaviors, and behaviors with customers. A few studies are beginning to explore modifying quality performance, such as reducing production errors and rework.[3]

Organizational behavior modification (OBM) is essentially a problem-solving approach to improving behavior. It consists of a series of steps.

1. *Define the target behavior.* Define the problem behavior at hand as specific behaviors that are observable and measurable.

2. *Take a baseline of the behavior in its natural state.* Graph the frequency of behavior over a period of time to understand its variability.

3. *Do a functional analysis.* Analyze antecedents and consequences in the environment that can control the behavior.

4. *Intervene with a reinforcement program.* Use some combination of reinforcers to attempt to increase the target behavior.

5. *Evaluate the program.* Graph the results and compare them to the baseline data to determine that behavior actually improved.

OBM Parallels to TQM

We can see many parallels between OBM and TQM that were pointed out as early as 1987 in a special issue of the *Journal of Organizational Behavior Management*.[4] Both programs focus on measurable variables and are data-driven. Both analyze causes (functional analysis in OBM; common and special causes in TQM). Both are essentially problem-solving approaches to improving behavior. We will hopefully see collaborative efforts between OBM practitioners and TQM managers in the near future.

TQM Motivational Principles Derived from Reinforcement Theory

- *Contingency.* Make rewards contingent on desirable behaviors. Follow the reward as immediately after the behavior as possible. Give bonuses on the spot rather than months after the accomplishment. Ensure that the individual or team associates the reward with the behavior being rewarded through a direct communication or a written statement to that effect. An article in the company newsletter or a formal award presentation can serve this function.

- *Valued rewards.* Individual employees and teams have their own prior reinforcement history that dictates preferences for certain rewards. Some may prefer cash; others may prefer symbols, such as signs or plaques. Still others may prefer a public forum, like a quality fair, where they can receive public recognition for their efforts. Be sure that you are aware of preferences for rewards.

Employee and quality team participation in setting awards ensures that individual preferences will be taken into account.

EXPECTANCY THEORY

Another approach to motivation is expectancy theory. It is considered a cognitive theory because it defines motivation in terms of people's perceptions and beliefs about how their efforts are related to subsequent events. Expectancy theory assumes that people are rational beings who, when faced with a certain course of action, determine their motivation to take that action based on their perception of the possible success of that action and the probability of occurrence of various outcomes that they value. This somewhat convoluted definition can be better understood if we break down expectancy theory into its components and then examine how the components fit together. Expectancy theory consists of three concepts: expectancy, instrumentality, and valence.[5]

Expectancy

Expectancy (E) is the person's subjective probability that the course of action he or she is considering will result in success. Like any probability, E ranges from 0 (no probability of success) to 1.0 (perfect probability of success). It is a subjective probability because it is based on what the person perceives is the chance of success, which may or may not be the actual probability of success. For example, the supervisor asks a salesperson to sell half again as much of the product as the salesperson usually sells. The salesperson might think, "That's no problem at all," which would translate into $E = 1.0$. Or, the salesperson might think, "That's difficult but doable with hard work," which is essentially a statement of $E = 0.5$. Or, the salesperson might think, "There's no way to do this," which means $E = 0$.

Instrumentality

The person also thinks how that action he or she is considering relates to various outcomes that might occur because of that effort; this is the instrumentality (I) of the action for making various rewards occur. An action, such as selling a certain amount of a product, will have several possible rewards linked to it, such as a bonus, a promotion, or time off. Each of these rewards has a certain *I* in the mind of the person linked to the action. In our sales example, the salesperson might think, "If I sell that amount, the chance of getting a bonus is pretty good" (*I* = 0.7); "The chance of getting a promotion is nil because hardly anyone gets promoted around here for any kind of effort" (*I* = 0); or "The chance of getting time off is possible—some seem to get it, some don't" (*I* = 0.5).

There are a couple of important points about instrumentality to consider here. Notice that the perception of instrumentality is linked to the person's perceptions of how the organization dispenses various rewards. If the organization is perceived to be consistent and equitable in giving out rewards, instrumentalities will be fairly high. On the other hand, if the organization is haphazard, inconsistent, and unfair in distributing rewards, employee instrumentalities will be much lower. Also notice that the concept of instrumentality as consistency is close to the reinforcement theory concept of contingency.

Valence

Each of these outcomes has a certain value or valence (*V*) to the person. Notice that this concept is similar to the concept of valued reward in reinforcement theory. Similar to reinforcement theory, expectancy theory states that people have individual differences in how they value rewards. Each possible reward will have a different valence to the person. In our sales example, the salesperson might value a bonus highly (*V* = 9 on a 10-point scale), a promotion as not too important (*V* = 3), and time off as somewhat important (*V* = 5).

Expectancy Equation

According to expectancy theory, these three concepts are related in the following equation.

$$\text{Motivation} = E \times \sum (I \times V)$$

Graphically this would look like Figure 3.2.

The obvious advantage of expectancy theory is that a researcher could survey employees for the values of *E*, *I*, and *V* for various courses of action, plug those numbers into the equation, get a prediction of

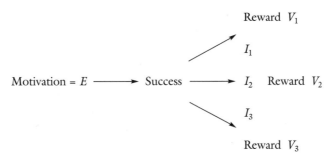

FIGURE 3.2. Expectancy theory model.

the employee motivation toward each course of action, and then check the prediction against what the employees actually did. In other words, expectancy theory allows tests of its predictions. Consequently, it has been well researched by academicians.

But what does this mean for practicing managers? It is not feasible to survey employees about their E, I, and V every time a manager wishes to know employee motivation to do something. Rather, the importance of expectancy theory as an applied theory lies in the nature of its equation. Notice that the equation is a multiplicative relationship of expectancy, instrumentality, and valence. This means that increasing any of the three variables should increase motivation according to expectancy theory. The importance to the practicing manager then lies in how to increase E, I, and V.

Increasing Expectancy. Employees' perception of their expectancy of success of a certain action can be enhanced several ways.

- *Training.* Training will increase employees' ability to do the task. With more ability, people should believe they are more apt to succeed on a task. Note that extensive training is an integral part of TQM activities. Two of Deming's 14 principles involve training. In addition, Juran advocates extensive skills training in his quality approach.[6]

- *Communication.* Supervisory "pep talks" can enhance employees' confidence that they can succeed at a task. In other words, the TQM manager can serve as a coach who builds greater confidence in the employee that should translate into greater perceived chances of success in the employee.

- *Empowerment.* TQM managers giving employees the power to accomplish tasks by giving them the authority to make important decisions about the task and the resources to back those decisions should increase employees' perception that they will succeed. Moreover, empowerment is a basic principle of TQM.

- *Prior experience.* Past experience with similar tasks through appropriate job assignments should increase employee knowledge of how to do the task. Experience should build expectancy of success.

- *Team effort.* Theoretically, a well-functioning team with its increased pool of information and ways of accomplishing tasks should be more effective than even a highly capable individual. The quality team efforts in TQM should thus increase employees' perceptions that even difficult tasks are doable.

Increasing Instrumentality.   We already saw that individuals' instrumentality depends on how they perceive the organization to run its reward system. Employees should have higher instrumentalities if they work in organizations that are consistent in their rewards process; that is, rewards are given immediately following good performance and are perceived as fair and equitable. Personal communications, articles in newsletters, and formal presentations can all enhance instrumentality.

Increasing Valence.   Valence is largely a function of individual preferences that have already been set. Managers can influence valence, however, in two ways.

1. *Induce change in valence.* TQM managers can "talk up" the importance of rewards that are within their power to dispense, such as flexible work scheduling and interesting work assignments.

2. *Introduce new rewards.* Because the expectancy equation sums the product of I and V of various rewards, motivation can theoretically be increased by adding new rewards that add additional I and V products to the equation. TQM managers can introduce new rewards to employees that are within the managers' power to confer, such as time off, new work schedules, and new quality awards.

   Indeed, employee quality teams could perhaps introduce even more highly valent rewards than managers could. Teams composed of employees themselves would best know the value of new rewards that could be conferred on themselves and fellow employees. Further, teams would best know what rewards would be valued as team rewards. Finally, teams could pool individual employee knowledge bases for creating new and highly valued rewards.

TQM Motivational Principles Derived from Expectancy Theory

- *TQM training increases expectancy of success.* TQM emphasizes extensive training that should improve employee ability to accomplish TQM tasks.

- *Empowerment increases expectancy of success.* Allowing individuals and quality teams the ability to make important decisions and giving them the resources to back those decisions should increase employee chances of success.

- *Team effort increases expectancy of success.* Employees pooling their individual knowledge bases, experience, and expertise in quality teams should increase the chances of task success.

- *Consistency in the organizational reward process increases instrumentality that success leads to rewards.* A TQM organization that is fair, consistent, and immediate in its reward system increases employee perceptions that their efforts will consistently lead to rewards. This is another manifestation of the organizational constancy that Deming insisted that a TQM organization must possess.[7]

- *Team input into creating the reward system increases valence of rewards.* Employee teams would know the most valent rewards for individual employees and employee teams. Moreover, teams could pool individual employee ideas for new and innovative rewards that could be highly valent.

GOAL-SETTING THEORY

Goal setting is a proven means of motivation in an organization. There are a large number of empirical studies that demonstrate its effectiveness. Indeed, some believe that goal-setting theory should be elevated to the status of a law in management.[8]

Deming and Goals

Before proceeding, we should discuss Deming's views toward goals. Deming was against goal setting in the context of MBO and merit pay, because he believed that this type of goal setting serves to focus on the individual rather than the organization.[9] Instead of emphasizing organizational values of quality and improvement, the individual strives to further him- or herself. Competition abounds; the organizational mission of quality improvement is ignored.

Deming, however, was not against all goal setting. He believed that goals, such as strategic planning, that further the organization's drive toward quality are acceptable. Therefore, goal setting that fosters quality performance can be a motivational technique.

Goal-Setting Model

Much of the recent research on goal setting has been carried out by Edwin A. Locke and his colleagues. In a well-cited article, he lays out a model of how the variables involved in goal setting affect performance. An abbreviated version of that model identifying variables important for TQM performance appears in Figure 3.3.[10]

We now look at how each set of variables in turn promotes quality performance.

Input Variables

- *Employee participation.* Participation increases motivation in two ways. First, it allows employees to become actively involved in

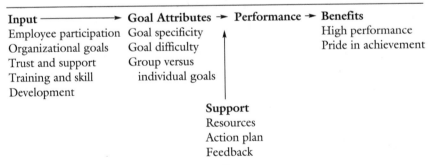

FIGURE 3.3. Goal-setting model adapted from Latham and Locke. Reprinted, by permission of publisher, from *Organizational Dynamics,* Autumn/1979. ©1979. American Management Association, New York. All rights reserved.

the goal-setting process, which creates in them a sense of owner-ship of the process and of the results of quality improvement. Process ownership is an important feature of TQM. Second, participation allows the pooling of individual employee information about what goals to strive for and how to reach them. Further, the process of participation itself may bring out new information that employees did not possess before.[11]

- *Organizational goals.* The strategic plan sets the overall mission of the organization toward quality and continuous improvement. Quality goals then filter down through the organization.

- *Trust and support.* An environment of trust allows the free exchange of information in order to reach goals. In this environment, supportive managers serve as facilitators who help individuals and teams reach their goals.

- *Training and skill development.* Training and skill development efforts improve employee and team abilities to reach difficult and challenging goals and at the same time provide confidence that the goals will be reached.

Goal Attributes

- *Goal specificity.* There is a large amount of empirical research that shows that specific data-based goals are more effective than general goals (such as, "Do your best").[12] Specific goals (for example, increase customer satisfaction ratings 20 percent) allow individuals and teams to measure their progress toward the goal.

- *Goal difficulty.* There is also a large amount of empirical evidence demonstrating that difficult, but not impossible, goals provide challenge that motivates people to strive toward these goals.[13]

- *Group versus individual goals.* Group goals enhance cooperation and team spirit. In addition, highly interdependent tasks (performing one task depends on the coordinated completion of other tasks) lend themselves well to group goals. Many TQM tasks, such as solving quality problems, are interdependent and cross-functional and, thus, would be enhanced by group goals.

Support

- *Resources.* Employees must have resources—such as money, equipment, and freedom—to make decisions, in order to reach goals. This is basically a statement that employees must be empowered in order to reach challenging goals.

- *Action plan.* The action plan specifies procedures for meeting goals. Deming emphasized the use of an action plan in his 14th principle.[14]
- *Feedback.* Specific feedback on performance shows employees and teams how close they are coming to reaching the goal, so they can adjust their level of performance if they are off course. Feedback can come from the work supervisors, peers, and internal and external customers.

Benefits

- *High performance.* There is extensive evidence that goal setting results not only in higher productivity but also in higher-quality performance.[15]
- *Pride in achievement.* Meeting challenging (difficult and specific) goals enhances pride in achievement. This is similar to Deming's principle of pride in work.[16]

TQM Motivational Principles Derived From Goal-Setting Theory

- *Employee participation improves quality performance.* Participation provides both a sense of ownership of the process and a pool of information for meeting the performance goal.
- *Organizational TQM goals drive individual and team goals.* The organizational strategic plan sets the basic direction of the organization on the course of quality improvement. TQM goals then filter down to quality teams and individuals.
- *Climate of trust and support enhances quality performance.* A climate of trust and support allows employees to feel free to propose suggestions and make decisions to improve quality. Supervisors in such a climate serve as facilitators to help individuals and teams meet quality goals.
- *Training improves quality performance.* Training in technical skills and TQM skills serves to increase ability and confidence in order to reach TQM goals.
- *Challenging goals enhance pride in performance.* Specific and difficult goals provide challenge to motivate employees and groups to meet these goals. Reaching such challenging goals instills a pride in performance.

- *Team goals enhance teamwork toward quality improvements.* Team goals enhance cooperation and team spirit necessary for teams to work together to reach quality goals. Team goals also bring people from different areas together to meet goals. Team goals should thus help to accomplish Deming's principle of breaking down barriers.[17]

- *Feedback improves quality performance.* Specific feedback from supervisors, peers, and customers gives employees and teams knowledge about how closely they are coming to reaching the goal.

JOB CHARACTERISTICS MODEL

The job characteristics model states that aspects of the job itself can improve worker motivation by enhancing the critical internal psychological states of experienced meaningfulness of the work (work is important, valuable, and worthwhile), experienced responsibility for work results, and knowledge of the actual results of the work.[18] This model nicely incorporates the essence of traditional theories of work motivation, such as Frederick Herzberg's idea that job enrichment provides motivators to improve worker performance, which Juran advocates in his quality control handbook.[19]

There are five job dimensions that motivate the worker through enhancing the internal psychological states.

Skill Variety. The worker must use different skills to perform the variety of tasks needed by the work. Skill variety can be increased if TQM managers

- *Combine tasks.* By combining tasks into a larger work unit, the worker can get away from specialized small work units and do something more meaningful.

- *Establish client relations.* When workers are allowed to deal directly with customers, they must develop a variety of interpersonal and problem-solving skills in order to better serve their customers.

Task Identity. When the worker does a meaningful whole piece of work, he or she develops an identity with a job well-done. In Deming's terms, pride of work develops. Task identity can be increased if TQM managers

- *Combine tasks.* Doing a number of tasks allows the worker to see the product come together into a meaningful whole.
- *Form natural work units.* Combining tasks into natural work units, which have a logical, meaningful sequence, allows workers to develop a sense of ownership of the unit. Ownership of work processes is a primary principle of TQM.

Task Significance. Task significance means that employees do work that is considered to be important by both peers and clients (internal and external customers). Task significance is enhanced if TQM managers

- *Form natural work units.* Natural work units have been arranged in a meaningful sequence that demonstrates its importance to the worker.

Autonomy.   Autonomy is the freedom of the worker to arrange work schedules and make decisions to get the job done. Autonomy is increased by

- *Vertical loading.* The TQM manager delegates some of his or her responsibility for work scheduling, planning, and decision making to the workers.

Feedback.   Direct, specific feedback on work progress gives workers clear information about task performance. Feedback is improved by

- *Open feedback channels.* Traditional quality control by inspecting products after they had been manufactured removed direct feedback of performance from the worker. There are several channels that can return feedback to the worker—work itself (seeing the product come together), peer comments, and supervisor comments. This is basically a restatement of Deming's principle of removing blocks to information needed by the worker.[20] Moreover, tools such as SPC can supply direct performance feedback to the worker.
- *Client relationships.* A primary source of information is the customer. Direct access to the customer allows the worker direct feedback on customer satisfaction with the product.

TQM Motivational Principles Derived from the Job Characteristics Model

- *TQM training enhances skill variety.* Workers must possess skill variety in order to perform multiple work tasks. TQM training can provide a number of statistical and problem-solving skills.

- *Reward and recognition enhance task significance and feedback.* Rewards, awards, and other types of recognition provide visible signs that the work is important. Moreover, reward and recognition provide direct feedback that workers are performing well.

- *Presenting TQM efforts to others enhances task significance.* Allowing workers and teams to present their TQM successes to peers and groups outside the company reinforces their pride in work; they are doing important work.

- *Customer contact enhances skill variety and feedback.* Workers need interpersonal and problem-solving skills to deal with customer problems. Customer contact gives them direct feedback on their work performance.

SUMMARY OF MOTIVATIONAL PRINCIPLES FOR TQM

Motivation in organizations must be managed if it is to be effective. Like any other organization, the TQM organization must manage the motivation of individual employees as well as quality teams. The various motivation principles we have examined are highlighted here.

- Consistency in the organizational reward process increases perceived contingency (instrumentality) that success leads to rewards.

- Rewards must be valued (valent) by employees and teams.

- TQM training increases expectancy of TQM task success and skill variety.

- Empowerment increases expectancy of TQM task success and autonomy.

- Team effort increases expectancy of success.

- Team input into creating the reward system increases valence of rewards.
- Employee participation improves quality performance.
- Organizational TQM goals drive individual and team goals.
- A climate of trust and support enhances quality performance.
- Challenging goals enhance pride in performance.
- Team goals enhance teamwork toward quality improvements.
- Feedback improves quality performance.
- Reward and recognition enhance task significance and feedback.
- Presenting TQM efforts to others enhances task significance.
- Customer contact enhances skill variety and feedback.

NOTES

1. Richard M. Steers and Lyman W. Porter, *Motivation and Work Behavior,* 5th ed. (New York: McGraw-Hill, 1991).

2. B. F. Skinner, *Contingencies of Reinforcement* (New York: Appleton-Century-Crofts, 1969).

3. Summaries of OBM research occur in Fred Luthans and Robert Kreitner, *Organizational Behavior Modification and Beyond* (Glenview, Ill.: Scott, Foresman, 1985); Kirk O'Hara, C. Merle Johnson, and Terry A. Beehr, "Organizational Behavior Management in the Private Sector: A Review of Empirical Research and Recommendations for Further Investigation," *Academy of Management Review* 10 (1985): 848–64.

4. Thomas C. Mawhinney, ed., "Special Issue on Organizational Behavior Management and Statistical Process Control: Theory, Technology, and Research" *Journal of Organizational Behavior Management* 9, no. 1 (1987): 1–156.

5. Victor H. Vroom, *Work and Motivation* (New York: Wiley, 1964); Craig C. Pinder, *Work Motivation* (Glenview, Ill.: Scott, Foresman, 1984); James R. Evans and William M. Lindsay, *The Management and Control of Quality,* 2d ed. (Minneapolis, Minn.: West, 1993).

6. W. Edwards Deming, *Out of the Crisis* (Cambridge, Mass.: MIT Center for Advanced Engineering Study, 1986), 23–24; J. M. Juran, *Juran's Quality Control Handbook,* 4th ed. (New York: McGraw-Hill, 1988), 11.1–11.39.

7. Deming, *Out of the Crisis,* 24.

8. Anthony J. Mento, Robert P. Steel, and Ronald J. Karren, "A Meta-Analytic Study of the Effects of Goal Setting on Task Performance," *Organizational Behavior and Human Decision Processes* 39 (1987): 52–83.

9. Deming, *Out of the Crisis,* 102.

10. Gary P. Latham and Edwin A. Locke, "Goal Setting—A Motivational Technique that Works," *Organizational Dynamics* (Autumn 1979): 68–80.

11. Edwin A. Locke and David M. Schweiger, "Participation in Decision Making," in *Research in Organizational Behavior,* vol. 1, ed. Barry M. Staw (Greenwich, Conn.: JAI Press, 1978).

12. Mento, Steel, and Karren, "Effects of Goal Setting."

13. Ibid.

14. Deming, *Out of the Crisis,* 86.

15. Mento, Steel, and Karren, "Effects of Goal Setting."

16. Deming, *Out of the Crisis,* 77.

17. Ibid.

18. J. Richard Hackman, "Work Design," in *Improving Life at Work,* ed. J. Richard Hackman and J. L. Suttle (Glenview, Ill.: Scott, Foresman, 1977); J. Richard Hackman and Greg R. Oldham, *Work Redesign* (Reading, Mass.: Addison Wesley, 1980); Evans and Lindsay, *The Management and Control of Quality.*

19. Juran, *Juran's Quality Control Handbook,* 10.37–10.39.

20. Deming, *Out of the Crisis,* 62.

Chapter 4

Organizational Examples of the Reward and Recognition Process

For the long run, the motivation for quality should be built into the overall fabric of employee . . . relations.
　　　　　—J. M. Juran, *Juran's Quality Control Handbook*

The broadened human roles called for under TQM require a compatibly broad reward and recognition system.
—Richard J. Schonberger, "Total Quality Management Cuts a Broad Swath through Manufacturing and Beyond"

An increasingly large number of organizations are implementing TQM. Each has a somewhat different approach reflecting its particular mentor (Deming, Juran, or Crosby), its size, its technology, and the unique needs of its customers. Accordingly, each organization has evolved a somewhat different reward and recognition process. This chapter does not attempt to show a representative sampling of companies from various industrial sectors, but rather the organizations described here demonstrate the rich variety in effective reward and recognition techniques that various organizations have developed. These highly varied types of reward and recognition demonstrate a number of motivational principles examined in chapter 3.

MANUFACTURING SECTOR

TQM originated in the manufacturing sector where companies suddenly found themselves trying to compete with quality products in the United States and abroad.[1] Several typical examples follow.

Appleton Papers

Appleton Papers decided to decentralize its reward and recognition process in order to make rewards more personal and immediate. Consequently, each line manager has a recognition budget from which he or she can reward quality behaviors by buying gifts that individual employees would value, such as personalized items, jewelry, and surprise gifts.[2]

Granite Rock

Granite Rock, a small manufacturer of road construction materials, won the 1992 Baldrige Award. Each employee maps out skill development goals with his or her supervisor in the *Individual Professional Development Plan*. These goals are then used to plan company-wide skills training. Among recognition devices used by Granite Rock are individual and team awards given on Recognition Day and monetary Incentive Recognition Awards given for excellence beyond normal job duties.

Granite Rock has determined that the *Individual Professional Development Plan* and recognition awards have contributed to a 30 percent higher productivity level (measured by revenue per employee) than the national industry average. In addition, employee surveys show that Granite Rock employees are more satisfied in every category than national averages.[3]

Johnsonville Foods

Johnsonville Foods links company-wide profit sharing to company performance. Most important, employees designed the system and now run it. The cycle begins with employees who get together with their supervisors and arrive at a performance rating based on self-evaluation and supervisor evaluation. A profit-sharing team then calculates an average profit share of pretax profits based on total ratings. Employees in the top performance rating get 125 percent of the share, while employees receive 110 percent, 100 percent, 90 percent, and 75 percent shares, respectively, for the other performance ratings.

In addition, Johnsonville Foods does not give automatic cost-of-living or seniority raises. Rather, employees receive salary raises for developing skills and then taking on roles of increased responsibility in the TQM program.[4]

Lou Ana Foods

Lou Ana Foods, which makes the cooking oil used in many Cajun foods, has a year-end bonus based on profitability for all employees. In addition, there is a Nathan Frank Award ($1000) to the employee who best exemplifies total quality. During National Quality Month, Lou Ana has an annual Total Quality Fest, where each quality team displays project boards documenting its work.

Quality awards are also presented at the Total Quality Fest in a railroad motif. There is a Crewman's Award conferred on a peer by fellow employees. There is a Brakeman's Award for a team or individual whose project best demonstrates waste reduction. And, there is a Chairman's Award for overall outstanding team.

Lou Ana has a suggestion program for teams. Figure 4.1 shows the suggestion form, and Figure 4.2 is a flowchart of how the suggestion system operates. There is a $5 cash incentive for each team member for each suggestion implemented. In addition, there is a quarterly emphasis program where an additional bonus is given, above the $5 base, and prizes (tickets and gifts) are also awarded. In a recent year, Lou Ana received 47.7 suggestions per employee—96 percent of those suggestions were implemented.[5]

Motorola

Motorola developed a quality program early in the 1980s as a response to competition. Consequently, Motorola was one of the first Baldrige Award winners in 1988. In order to let its quality teams present their accomplishments in a competitive environment, Motorola puts on a Total Customer Satisfaction Team Competition (Quality Olympics) where teams from around the world present their quality efforts for gold, silver, or bronze medals. Figure 4.3 shows the competition scoring criteria. Teams are evaluated in seven categories: teamwork, project selection, analysis techniques, remedies, results, institutionalization, and presentation. Motorola prints a booklet each year containing a color picture of the members of each finalist team, the team name, and a summary of the team project. In 1993, about 4400 teams competed worldwide for 24 slots in the finals (6 gold and

The Schad Industries Suggestion Form

Submitter/Team _____ Date _____

Team members and nos. _____

Idea _____

_____

_____

_____

Benefits of idea/justification _____

_____

Feel free to add pages, sketches, drawings, process flowcharts, diagrams.

Team feedback

__ Being   __ On hold   __ Not to be used   Sent to dept. head   Team leader _____
   implemented   (Please explain   (Please explain   __ Over $250 limit   Date _____
   by team   below)   below)   __ Other (Explain)

Comments _____

_____

Department head—Review required within 10 days of team approval

__ Approved   __ On hold   __ Not to be used   Sent to CEO   Team leader _____
             (Please explain   (Please explain   __ Over $1000 limit   Date _____
             below)   below)   __ Strategic project

Comments _____

_____

CEO—Review required within 30 days of department head approval

__ Approved   __ On hold   __ Not to be used   CEO _____
             (Please explain   (Please explain   Date _____
             below)   below)

Comments _____

_____

Recognition committee suggestion control no. _____ Date _____

FIGURE 4.1. Lou Ana Foods suggestion form. Source: Lou Ana Foods. Reprinted with permission.

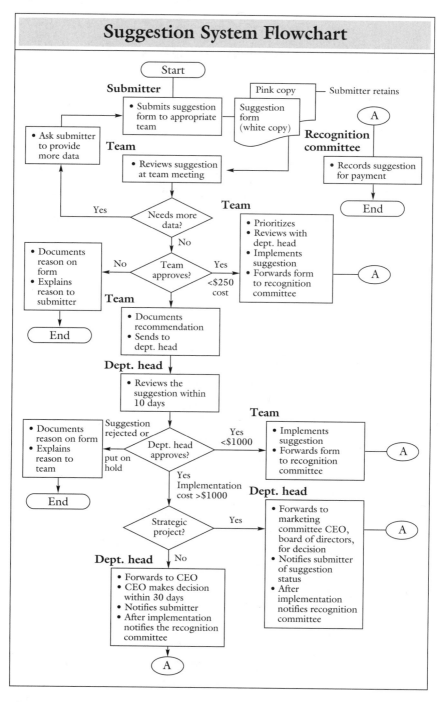

FIGURE 4.2. Lou Ana Foods suggestion system flowchart. Source: Lou Ana Foods. Reprinted with permission.

MOTOROLA INC.
CORPORATE T.C.S. TEAM COMPETITION FORM

Organization: Date _____

Team Name:

Key Initiative	Total Cycle Time		Participative Management	
	Profit Improvement		Six Sigma Quality	Product Mfg. Leadership

Category	Criteria	Score 0 to 10	Weight	Weighted Score
Teamwork	• Appropriate team structure and membership • Participation by all members • Understanding and use of group dynamics		1	
Project Selection Criteria	• Criteria and methodology evident in selection • Identification of customer and his or her needs • Clear and aggressive goals established		1	
Analysis Techniques	• Appropriate analytical techniques are used • Customer's needs are considered • Growth in team's knowledge and skill with tools		2	
Remedies	• Alternatives explored, implementations thorough • Containment vs. root cause prevention is clear • Enhancements or improvements were made • Innovation in the remedies or implementation		2	
Results	• Results reflect goals and difficulty of project • Ancillary effects identified and evaluated • Results verified and documented		2	
Institutionalization	• Improvements sustainable and permanent • Improvements have application in other areas • Grasp of concept of continuous improvement		1	
Presentation	• Clear, concise, follows the process • Skillful, appropriate use of presentation aids		1	
			Weighted Score	
Time (minutes)		Deductions (–1 point for each minute > 12)		
			Total Team Score	
Judge				
Comments				
2/20/92				11

FIGURE 4.3.   Motorola Total Customer Satisfaction Team Competition criteria. Source: Motorola. Reprinted with permission.

18 silver medals). Judges for the final competition were Motorola's CEO and senior executives.

In addition, individuals and groups compete for the CEO Quality Award, the highest award at Motorola. A top executive (CEO, chief operating officer [COO], or president) will fly anywhere in the world to present the award. One employee won the award with more than 200 suggestions for improvements implemented.[6]

Star Enterprises

Star Enterprises, a subsidiary of Texaco, has an elaborate visible system of tokens and rewards. Each TQM team has a distinctive T-shirt, and the organization has a mascot, Qualigator, an individual in an alligator suit. Star Enterprises encourages its teams to become involved with quality improvement efforts in surrounding communities and to take their dynamic team presentations using their TQM T-shirts and alligator mascot on the road.[7]

Storage Technology Corporation

Storage Technology Corporation (StorageTek) manufactures information storage subsystems for large computers. The reward and recognition team meets weekly to benchmark other organizations. As a result, StorageTek has a variety of offerings. Individuals can win the Outstanding Contribution Award, Technical Excellence Award, and Chairman's Quality Award. Teams can win the Outstanding Performance Award. These awards are supplemented by recognition in the form of gifts, certificates, letters of commendation, dinners, and trips for off-site career enhancement.

The top 36 executives at StorageTek share their management objectives as a team. Their annual bonus depends on meeting these shared goals.

Performance appraisal for employees is being replaced by personal development reviews. Employee pay will consist of competency pay for acquired skills and knowledge and performance pay (variable one-time cash awards for quality performance). A pilot gain sharing program allocates cash bonuses for production improvements and cost savings.

StorageTek pays employees at the 90th to 95th percentile of its industry. With such a high pay base, StorageTek calculates that even a 5 percent average pay increase to its entire work force will ultimately cost several million dollars. Consequently, it is looking to recoup pay increases through increased profitability and reduced costs company-wide. On the other hand, recognition costs are much lower and are funded through savings from local department budgets.[8]

Stuller Settings

Stuller Settings is a jewelry manufacturer in Lafayette, Louisiana, and recently won the U.S. Senate Productivity Award for its innovation and quality. In a labor-intensive industry, Stuller knew it had to try new methods to survive. To counter the tight security it must maintain (and the windowless work area), Stuller gave employees great leeway in decorating their work areas to suit their own tastes. Because Lafayette does not have a jewelry center as does New York City, Stuller must hire inexperienced employees and train them to be jewelry makers. As each employee completes a training or cross-training unit, he or she receives a certificate in a formal presentation. The award presentation ceremonies have become an integral part of Stuller's corporate culture. Employees are encouraged to dress in costumes, such as Mardi Gras costumes, and humor is encouraged during the presentation.

Stuller has a cash awards program called Ideas Pay. Employees are encouraged to make written suggestions about improving the product, tools, handling of materials, equipment, or working conditions. They can also make suggestions on combining operations or eliminating unnecessary operations, reducing waste, and eliminating accident hazards. A suggestion committee evaluates these suggestions on possible savings and initiative and ingenuity. Awards start at $10 (one employee recently received a $1500 award for reclaiming gold). About 25 percent of the suggestions are implemented by management.[9]

Westinghouse

In 1979 Westinghouse determined that it had to be more competitive in the global market. It began to institute productivity improvements, but soon decided that the deciding factor was quality. In 1985 it developed a total quality program. In 1988 the Commercial Nuclear Fuel Division of Westinghouse won the first Baldrige Award. In 1989 Westinghouse initiated the George Westinghouse Total Quality Awards program, which is an internal competition among units modeled after the Baldrige Award. A board of examiners evaluates nominated units on Westinghouse's 12 conditions of excellence arrayed in four broad categories: management leadership (culture, planning, communications, and accountability), product/process leadership (products/services, processes/procedures, information, and suppliers), human resource excellence (participation, development, and motivation), and customer orientation.

Figure 4.4 shows the three factors used to evaluate the 12 conditions: approach (degree to which total quality is integrated across all functions), implementation (breadth and depth of implementation of the conditions throughout the organization), and results (quality and magnitude of achievements). Units that achieve the top band of the scoring guidelines in Figure 4.4 win the Chairman's Gold Award. Units at the next highest band win the Silver Award. Units that earn a site visit but do not win a Gold or Silver Award receive a Finalist Award. Units that are evaluated for awards receive an evaluation scorebook as feedback on their progress. Winners' and finalists' names are released to suppliers and government agencies with which Westinghouse does business.

Looking back on its experiences with quality and recognition, Westinghouse identified several hurdles it had to overcome.[10]

1. *Focus on symptoms.* Symptoms are visible numbers which invite managers to "slap on a patch" and then slap on a reward to someone. Long-term solutions depend on a focus on the process.

2. *Focus on experts.* Experts can suggest short-term ideas, but long-term improvements to systems, including reward and recognition, can come only from employee teams.

3. *Time.* Results take time—up to two years in some cases.

4. *Limited recognition.* Many existing acts of recognition have only short-term effects. The recognition program must be continuous, involving input from individuals, teams, and the organization.

5. *Recognition not linked to TQM culture.* Traditional corporate cultures do not focus on recognition. TQM culture, on the other hand, is "recognition rich" and requires involved employees, a focus on customers, and managers as enablers.

	Approach	Implementation	Results
	• Total quality process based • Breadth of integration across all functions • Innovation evident in approach	• Breadth of implementation (areas or functions) • Depth of implementation (ingrained in people)	• Quality of measurable results • Business payoff of the approach
100% Chairman's Gold Award	• World-class approach; sound, systematic, effective, total quality based; continuously evaluated, refined, and improved • Total integration across all functions • Proven innovations	• Fully in all areas and functions • Ingrained in the culture	• Exceptional, world-class, superior to all competition; in all areas • Sustained, business-related, results clearly caused by the approach
80% Silver Award	• Well developed and tested, total quality based • Excellent integration • Innovative	• In almost all areas and functions • Evident in the culture of all groups	• Excellent, sustained in all areas with improving business performance • Much evidence that results are caused by the approach
60%	• Well planned, documented, sound, systematic, total quality based; not all aspects addressed • Good integration • Approach is customized for business	• In most areas and functions • Evident in the culture of most groups	• Solid, business-related, with positive trends in most areas • Some evidence that results are caused by the approach
40%	• Beginning of sound, systematic, total quality based; not all aspects addressed • Fair integration	• Begun in many areas and functions • Evident in the culture of some groups	• Some successes in major areas • Not much evidence that results are caused by the approach
20%	• Beginning of total quality awareness • No integration across functions	• Beginning in some areas and functions • Not a part of the culture	• Few or no results • Little or no evidence that any results are caused by the approach
0%			

FIGURE 4.4.   Westinghouse Total Quality Awards scoring guidelines. Source: Westinghouse Electric Corporation, Productivity and Quality Center. Reprinted with permission.

Xerox Business Products and Services

Xerox Business Products and Services (BPS) Division won the 1989 Baldrige Award. Individual employees can receive the President's Award and Achievement Awards. Teams can win the Team Excellence Award and Excellence in Customer Satisfaction Award. There is a gain sharing program for quality improvements. In order to be promoted at Xerox, a manager must demonstrate that he or she is a "role model for quality" for employees; managers must encourage quality thinking and reward and recognize quality efforts.[11]

SERVICE SECTOR

Corning Information Services Division

At the Information Services Division (ISD) of Corning, about 90 percent of employees belong to a cross-functional self-managed team. Both individual and team efforts are recognized in the reward system. Teams evaluate themselves on meeting team objectives, while in the older, more developed teams, teams evaluate individual members. In addition, ISD is piloting a goal-sharing project that includes incentives for spending within budget, customer satisfaction, process improvement, and cost reduction.[12]

Federal Express

Federal Express, a 1990 Baldrige Award winner, allows supervisors to confer instant cash awards for quality efforts. There is a Golden Falcon Award for customer service and a Bravo Zulu Award (Naval signal flags for *BZ* or *well done*) for accomplishment. Executives can earn up to 40% of their salary as quality bonuses. As an indicator of the success of its reward and recognition programs, a survey indicated that during a five-year period 91 percent of employees are "proud to work for Federal Express."[13]

Florida Power and Light

Florida Power and Light began its TQM process with small monetary rewards and banquets for TQM improvement efforts. Relatively quickly, it found that employees resented these rewards as being too small and based too closely on the physical appearance of their TQM reports. Discussion groups showed that employees preferred to see their suggestions in action. Therefore, Florida Power and Light instituted an expo fair in which employees could demonstrate to other employees and the community their process improvement efforts. At the same time, it must be acknowledged that external factors can influence even good TQM practices. Florida Power and Light has recently had to curtail certain practices because of external economic pressures.[14]

IBM Marketing

An IBM marketing division commissioned a survey of its employees on its reward and recognition system. The survey showed that cash award recognition was viewed as compensation, employees and customers were not involved in the process, recognition was not linked to teamwork or customer satisfaction, recognition was not timely, and winners of recognition were not publicized. To improve the situation, IBM developed a four-part action plan.[15]

1. *Education.* A video and workbook were devised to train managers to use reward and recognition more effectively.

2. *Improve cash awards.* A trifecta concept developed a three-step cash award program: the cash award, a surprise gift sent to the employee's home, and an experience to remember the event (show tickets or dinner).

3. *Peer-to-peer award.* An employee or customer nominates a peer. The award recommender then receives $20 to buy a gift for the awardee.

4. *Market-driven quality award.* A team nominates another team for the award based on teamwork and use of quality tools and processes.

Marquette Bank Minneapolis

Thus far we have focused on reward and recognition of employees. Marquette Bank Minneapolis has taken the emphasis on customer satisfaction further and rewards the customer for feedback to the bank. A customer who points out a problem or error to the bank receives $5 as a reward. The bank tracks the reason for payment and payouts as a measure of customer satisfaction.[16]

PUBLIC SERVICE SECTOR

The public sector is increasingly embracing TQM. More than 60 percent of federal organizations are planning a TQM effort.[17]

City of Phoenix

The city of Phoenix, Arizona, has developed a version of TQM where a number of programs reward quality. A suggestion program rewards those who suggest ideas resulting in a savings to the city. There is a differentiation between tangible and intangible savings. Tangible savings result from a measurable cost reduction. Tangible savings are calculated by subtracting the first-year implementation cost (cost of equipment to implement the idea divided by the expected life of the improvement) from the first-year cost savings. The reward for a tangible savings suggestion is 10 percent of the first year's savings, up to $2500. During 1992 the employee suggestion program produced savings of $1,184,000.

Intangible savings, on the other hand, have no immediate measurable cost savings. Examples of intangible savings are making a job easier or more pleasant, improving employee safety, enhancing customer relations, and improving employee morale. Suggestions for intangible savings are rewarded with $25 to $500.

In addition, individuals and groups can win the City Manager's Excellence Award. Figure 4.5 shows that winners of the award are honored at a breakfast hosted by the mayor and city manager. The award ceremony is televised and a picture of the award winner is placed in a municipal building. City employees also can win certificates of commendation, plaques, and pins. The awards selection committee rewards contributions as well as deeds and tries to select a wide spectrum of winners each year in order to give broad recognition to quality efforts.[18]

Navy Supply Center, San Diego

A recognition and reward PAT, composed of top managers and middle managers with employee representatives, monitors the reward system as a process within the Navy Supply Center in San Diego. Gain sharing monetary rewards are given to individuals and teams for special accomplishments. Recognition ceremonies are held.[19]

City of Phoenix
Excellence Award

City Manager's Award for Excellence in Public Service
This program, supported by City Manager Frank Fairbanks and Mayor Paul Johnson, recognizes employees and employee groups for exceptional contributions to city government and to the public.

Who can win?
Any city employee or employee group. An employee group could be a task force, a team, a squad, a crew, or any combination of people who work together on a project.

Nominations
Any employee at any level of city government may nominate any other employee or employee group for an award. Recipients of other city awards are also eligible for the Excellence Award. Volunteers and contracted employees are not eligible to receive this award.

Nominations will be screened by a special committee of city employees. The committee will determine the winners.

The criteria
Employees or employee groups would be eligible for the award after meeting one or more of the following:
- Continued and repeated excellence in overall job performance.
- Solving an extraordinary problem, achieving or exceeding a significantly difficult goal.
- Successful implementation of an innovative idea where the result was identifiable.
- Outstanding act which brings recognition to the city from the public.

Accomplishments should have been between August 1, 1992 and December 1, 1993.

The awards
Award recipients will be honored at an awards breakfast hosted by the mayor and city manager. Each winner may invite a guest—such as a spouse, supervisor, or friend—to this event.

Each winner will receive a commemorative award especially designed for this occasion. The Phoenix Channel (channel 11) will televise the event to promote community awareness of the excellence in city staff accomplishments.

Photographs of the winner in the work setting as well as with the mayor and city manager are also presented to each winner. A picture of each winner with a description of his or her performance will be displayed at the award ceremony and at major municipal buildings.

Nomination
The deadline for submitting Excellence Award nominations is December 17, 1993.

Nominator _____

Job Title _____

Dept. _____ Phone_____

Please follow the instructions on the back of this form to describe why the nominee deserves the Excellence Award. Be as specific as possible. Attach additional pages or other documentation as needed.
Note: Please keep nominations to a reasonable length and limit attachments to no more than 3 pages.

Return to:
Employee Development • Personnel Department
135 N. 2nd Avenue • Phoenix, Arizona 85003

FIGURE 4.5.   City of Phoenix City Manager's Excellence Award. Source: City of Phoenix. Reprinted with permission.

Oregon State University

During the 1980s, Oregon State University faced funding cuts of 35 percent from the state legislature while university operating costs continued to rise. In 1989 Oregon State began a TQM program as a means of managing shrinking resources, but at the same time maintaining quality education. Consequently, it has one of the most extensive TQM programs in higher education.

In its reward and recognition program, it gives three awards for individual and team performance based on time and money savings, uniqueness of solutions, and importance to the university. The Quality Award recognizes a significant problem-solving task. The Beaver Award (university mascot) recognizes continuous, high-quality work beyond goal expectations, such as special projects in addition to work on regular duties. The Great Performance Award is given for accomplishing a specific task beyond goal expectations, such as handling a crisis or correcting a problem that saves money. Accompanying the awards are plaques, money, and articles in the university newsletter. In addition, Oregon State has modeled a Quality Fair after Xerox, where teams can showcase their quality efforts.

Oregon State faced several challenges in implementing reward and recognition within a TQM framework. As in any university, faculty were highly independent and were accustomed to working at a largely individual level in teaching and research in order to receive faculty rewards of pay raises, tenure, and promotions. Faculty were also used to academic governance committees, which operate very differently from TQM teams focused on quality problems. Consequently, Oregon State recognizes that the evaluation criteria traditionally used for awarding raises, tenure, and promotion must be changed to support TQM by including continuous improvement efforts and work on TQM teams.[20]

Shawnee Mission Medical Center

Shawnee Mission Medical Center developed a personal development system to support TQM. Employees and supervisors first meet at the beginning of the evaluation year to identify three or four primary customers served by the employee. They then identify three to six key service areas that the employee's job covers. Next the employee and supervisor together set individual goals on improving service to the three or four primary customers of the employee. Employees and supervisors also jointly identify "challenge opportunities" that expand employee skills. During the evaluation year employees record accomplishments and solicit peer feedback on performance.

At the end of the period, the employee and supervisor discuss servicing key customers, goal accomplishments, and meeting challenge opportunities. Successfully meeting these criteria leads to a "contribution increase" (the same percentage for all employees). In addition, Shawnee Mission is developing a recognition system that incorporates time off, free travel, and dinner and theater tickets as awards.[21]

INTERNATIONAL SECTOR

Australia

Australia is in a unique position to serve as a Pacific Rim economic bridge between east and west. During a sabbatical in 1992 I studied the TQM programs of several Australian companies.

Amdahl Australia. The quality improvement process at Amdahl Australia, a computer services firm, formally recognizes individuals and groups with awards for quality contributions and accomplishments through its quality awareness committee. Among the awards are gifts, mementos, and cash for a night on the town, and a special cash award for a weekend on the town for a truly significant achievement.[22]

BHP Steel. Broken Hill Proprietary (BHP) is the largest company in Australia. BHP Steel emphasizes recognition systems. It writes up employee improvement projects in internal newspapers and magazines, and it encourages team presentations on quality improvements to top management. In addition, the rod and bar division operates a unique token economy called the Idea Development Employees Award Scheme (IDEAS). Employees gain points for quality team participation and for opportunities for improvement (identifying a problem or a means of improving a process). The points can then be traded in for restaurant dinners.[23]

Dow-Corning Australia. One of the older and more elaborate TQM programs in Australia is Dow-Corning Australia (DCA). One of the characteristics of its TQM program is continuous improvement of the TQM program itself. For example, DCA has added technical/process groups to its quality teams to handle the special quality problems of major process innovations. Similarly, its reward system has evolved as its TQM program has progressed. Initially, rewards included awards, plaques, and a quality medal. Over time, however, it was felt that these could be overused. Thus DCA now emphasizes public recognition of employee ideas; for example, sending employees to other firms and outside training. The emphasis, however, is still on immediate reward, even if only taking the employee to dinner. The quality council of DCA has a budget to dispense quality improvement rewards in a rapid and contingent fashion.[24]

State Bank of South Australia. State Bank of South Australia has implemented a service quality program that focuses on satisfaction of both external and internal customers. Moreover, it created customer listening groups to discern customer needs and problems. Its reward and recognition team required 12 months of listening to employees as internal customers concerning their problems with the organizational reward system. As State Bank evolved its service quality program, it moved from a traditional system based on seniority to a performance-based reward system. Among the problems was employee reluctance to move from the traditional seniority system, which focused on status rewards, to the more dynamic and contingent performance-based system, where external customer service was rewarded. The solution was an elaborate training program on quality service. Then customer-focused activities were rewarded by articles in internal publications and assignments to more challenging positions.[25]

China

Ford Lioho, Taiwan. According to Doug Rutherford, quality manager of Ford Australia who spent three years with Ford of Taiwan, quality circles are the basic structure of quality improvement in Taiwan as in other Asian countries. All employees belong to quality circles and reward is centered on the quality circle as a group rather than on individual members of the circle. There are modest monetary rewards given for improvement suggestions to the quality circle members. In addition, there are recognition awards bestowed on the quality circles, such as plaques and flags. More important, there is an annual competition in which the best quality circle from each area of the company is allowed to make a presentation of its efforts to top management.

Quality circles value this very highly; there is strong competition to be chosen as the best presentation.[26]

Germany

Messerschmidt-Boelkow-Blohm.   Messerschmidt-Boelkow-Blohm (MBB) purposely built its aircraft, missile, and research and development manufacturing operations at one site in order to ensure exchange of ideas on design and production. MBB has a formal employee suggestion system for improving manufacturing technology and increasing cost savings. Every suggestion is seriously considered, and significant improvement suggestions receive a financial award and a write-up in company publications.[27]

Great Britain

British Aerospace.   British Aerospace has organized commercial aircraft manufacturing operations into employee cells responsible for their own processes. British Aerospace holds a Quality Day where the employee teams receive prizes for quality improvement efforts.[28]

Japan

The Japanese tend to view motivation differently than Western countries. According to Ishikawa, one of the influential forces in Japanese total quality control, worker pay is tied to seniority and is not considered the most important motivator. Rather, Japanese workers are more strongly motivated by the satisfaction of doing a job well, the happiness arising from cooperating with others and from being recognized by others, and the joy of personal growth.[29] Recognition is thus important, but focuses on the group effort, such as prizes won by one's quality circle.

Suzuki Motor Company.   Suzuki has had quality circles for a number of years. After their initiation, the circles declined in effectiveness for a time. Management then decided to institute an evaluation system, in which circles where rated on number of suggestions, length of time the circle met, attendance at the circle meetings, amount of money saved from circle suggestions, and publication of suggestions at conferences. Various awards were given for evaluation scores ranging from the President's Prize to prizes for efforts. The recognition derived from winning these prizes was evidently highly motivating for "circles were not back-ward about receiving prizes."[30]

SUMMARY

Table 4.1 summarizes the reward and recognition characteristics of these organizations. It must be reiterated that this sample was not meant to be representative of TQM practices overall, but rather was meant to be illustrative of what organizations are doing (and also some of the problems they face). Given this caution, several points arise when examining Table 4.1.

Focus. The majority of organizations have both individual employee and employee team rewards and awards. One organization even re-wards customers.

Monetary Rewards. Cash bonuses are common. Some organizations are experimenting with gain sharing and profit sharing.

Types of Recognition. Plaques appear to be the most popular type of recognition award. There is a diversity in type of award, however—awards from important persons in the organization, such as the CEO, awards for accomplishments, awards for suggestions, awards for quali-ty, and awards for customer satisfaction. Formal presentations, such as dinners, and items in company publications frequently accompany the conferring of the award.

Motivation Principles. Many of the motivational principles pre-sented in chapter 3 are used by these organizations. The principle of contingency from reinforcement theory (or instrumentality from expectancy theory) is common. The awards are given soon after the effort or accomplishment occurs, and the award is associated with the good performance through a formal presentation or a news item in a company newsletter. Several organizations have some variation of a quality fair in which employees can publicly showcase their TQM efforts.

Many organizations allow employees to participate in creating and running the reward and recognition program through special teams. They thus emphasize the concept of valent rewards from expectancy theory. Moreover, some organizations use customer input, including feedback, in selecting award winners.

Some organizations integrate their goal-setting process with their reward and recognition process. Employees participate in setting TQM

TABLE 4.1.   Summary of the reward and recognition processes in TQM organizations.

Organization	Focus	Monetary share type	Recognition type	Special team	Motivational principles
Manufacturing					
Appleton Papers	Individual		Individualized gifts		Individually valued (valent) awards
Granite Rock	Individual and group	Incentive awards	Recognition Day awards		Skill development goals, public Recognition Day
Johnsonville Foods	Group	Profit sharing			Employee participation in rewards process, raises contingent on increased job responsibility, skill variety
Lou Ana Foods	Group	Bonus, prizes	Frank Award, Crewman's Award, Chairman's Award, Brakeman's Award, Total Qaulity Fest	Recognition team	Peer feedback in awards, team recognition at Quality Fest

Continued on next page

TABLE 4.1—Continued

Organization	Focus	Monetary share type	Recognition type	Special team	Motivational principles
Motorola	Individual and group	Quality Olympics, CEO Quality Award			Task significance through Quality Olympics, valent awards
Star Enterprises	Group		T-shirts, mascot	All employee teams	Employee participation disseminating TQM to community, task significance, valent awards
StorageTek	Individual and group	Competency pay, shared goals	Chairman's, Technical Excellence, Contribution, performance awards; commendations, gifts, trips	Reward and recognition team	Skill variety, shared goals, reward variety
Stuller Settings	Individual and group	Ideas Pay	Presentation ceremonies	Suggestion committee	Contingent awards, skill variety, participation in ceremonies

Continued on next page

TABLE 4.1—Continued

Organization	Focus	Monetary share type	Recognition type	Special team	Motivational principles
Westinghouse	Group		Gold, Silver, Finalist Awards	Award selection committee	Competition between units, feedback, customer recognition
Xerox BPS	Individual and group	Gain sharing	President's Award, Achievement Award, Team Excellence, Customer Satisfaction Award		Task significance through awards, contingent reward, managers as quality role models
Service					
Corning ISD	Individual and group	Incentives		Cross-functional teams	Team self-evaluation, goal sharing
Federal Express	Individual	Instant cash, salary bonus	Golden Falcon Award, Bravo Zulu Award		Contingent reward, customer feedback

Continued on next page

TABLE 4.1—Continued

Organization	Focus	Monetary share type	Recognition type	Special team	Motivational principles
Florida Power and Light	Group	Gain sharing	Banquet, expo fair	Discussion groups	Employee participation in setting reward and disseminating TQM information to community, team valent awards
IBM Marketing	Individual and group	Cash	Home gift experience, peer to peer award, quality award		Contingent awards, valent awards, customer feedback, peer participation
Marquette Bank	Customer	Cash for feedback			Contingent customer feedback
Public service					
City of Phoenix	Individual and group	Tangible/intangible savings, cash awards	Excellence awards, commendations	Award selection committee	Contingent cash award, variety of winners

Continued on next page

TABLE 4.1—Continued

Organization	Focus	Monetary share type	Recognition type	Special team	Motivational principles
Navy Supply Center	Individual and group	Gain sharing	Recognition ceremonies	Recognition and reward team	Rewards contingent on improvements and accomplishments
Oregon State University	Individual and group	Bonus	Quality Award, Beaver Award, Great Performance Award, newsletter, Quality Fair		Contingent awards, public presentation of efforts at Quality Fair
Shawnee Mission	Individual	Contribution increase	Time off, free travel, entertainment		Reward TQM skill development, challenge opportunities
International					
Amdahl Australia	Individual and group	Cash awards	Gift awards	Quality awareness committee	Awards contingent on contributions, valent rewards

Continued on next page

TABLE 4.1—Continued

Organization	Focus	Monetary share type	Recognition type	Special team	Motivational principles
BHP Steel	Individual and group		Articles in internal publications, presentations to top management		Valent rewards, team participation awards
Dow-Corning Australia	Individual and group	Cash awards	Plaque, awards, publicity, training	Financed by quality council	Contingent awards, reward skills training
State Bank of South Australia	Individual and group		Articles in internal publications, more challenging assignments	Reward and recognition team	Rewards contingent on customer service, participation in setting rewards, customer feedback
Ford Lioho Taiwan	Group	Cash awards	Plaques, flags, ceremonies	Quality circle	Competition for best presentation, valent awards

Continued on next page

TABLE 4.1—Continued

Organization	Focus	Monetary share type	Recognition type	Special team	Motivational principles
Messerschmidt-Boelkow-Blohm	Individual	Cash awards	Article in company publication		Participation in product design, valent awards
British Aerospace	Group	Prizes at Quality Day			Awards contingent on suggestions, participation in Quality Day
Suzuki	Group		President's Prize	Quality circle	Awards contingent on team efforts, competition for prizes, conference presentations

goals. Rewards are linked to meeting TQM goals. Some organizations are exploring goal sharing, while other organizations use competition for awards as a motivator. Some organizations have employees compete against themselves as challenge opportunities.

Several organizations reinforce training for skill variety (from the job characteristics model) in their reward and recognition program. Other organizations emphasize the importance of TQM tasks in their overall TQM program (task significance in the job characteristics model).

NOTES

1. Mary Walton, *Deming Management at Work* (New York: Putnam, 1990), 13.

2. Shari Caudron, "How HR Drives TQM," *Personnel Journal* (August 1993): 48B–48O.

3. Granite Rock, "Employee Performance and Recognition," section 4.4 in *Individual Professional Development Plan,* 1992 Baldrige Award application (Watsonville, Calif.: Granite Rock, 1993), 28–30.

4. Johnsonville Foods' CEO, Ralph C. Stayer, describes Johnsonville Foods' program in "How I Learned to Let My Workers Lead," *Harvard Business Review* (November 1990): 66–83; James A. Belasco and Ralph C. Stayer, *Flight of the Buffalo: Soaring to Excellence, Learning to Let Employees Lead* (New York: Warner Books, 1993).

5. Schad Industries, *Suggestion System* (Opelousas, La.: Schad Industries, 1993).

6. Motorola, *Total Customer Satisfaction Team Competition Criteria* (Schaumburg, Ill.: Motorola, 1992); Paul Noakes, Motorola vice president for external quality, telephone conversation with author, 5 January 1994.

7. Larry E. Arnold, "How to Keep the Momentum Going" (paper presented at the Louisiana Quality Symposium, Baton Rouge, La., October 1991).

8. A. Donald Stratton, "It's More than Statistics," *Quality Progress* 25 (July 1992): 71–72; StorageTek, *Rewards and Recognition Task Force Recommendations* (Louisville, Colo.: StorageTek, 1991).

9. Stuller Settings (Lafayette, La.: Stuller Settings, 1993).

10. Westinghouse Productivity and Quality Center, *The George Westinghouse Total Quality Awards* and *The Westinghouse Total Quality Experience* (Pittsburgh, Pa.: Westinghouse Productivity and Quality Center, 1993).

11. Richard Blackburn and Benson Rosen, "Total Quality and Human Resources Management: Lessons Learned from Baldrige Award–Winning Companies," *Academy of Management Executive* 7, no. 3 (August 1993): 49–66.

12. Harvey R. Shrednick, Richard J. Shutt, and Madeline Weiss, "Empowerment," *MIS Quarterly* 16 (1992): 491–505.

13. Blackburn and Rosen, "Baldrige Award–Winning Companies;" John J. Kendrick, "Customers Win in Baldrige Award Selections," *Quality* (January 1991): 23–31.

14. Mary Walton, *The Deming Management Method* (New York: Putnam, 1986), 24–82.

15. Brooks Carder and James D. Clark, "The Theory and Practice of Employee Recognition," *Quality Progress* 25 (December 1992): 25–30.

16. Anat Bird, "One Bank's Approach to Total Quality Management," *The Banker's Magazine* (May/June 1993): 63–68.

17. Albert C. Hyde, "The Proverbs of Total Quality Management: Recharting the Path to Quality Improvement in the Public Sector," *Public Productivity and Management Review* 16 (1992): 25–37.

18. City of Phoenix, *City of Phoenix Excellence Award Program Selection Committee Guide* and *Guide for Evaluating Employee Suggestions* (Phoenix, Ariz.: City of Phoenix, 1993).

19. Navy Supply Center, *Recognition Process Action Team Action Plan* (San Diego, Calif.: Navy Supply Center, 1991).

20. Larry E. Coate, "TQM at Oregon State University," *Journal for Quality and Participation* 13 (December 1990): 90–101; Larry E. Coate, *Total Quality Management at Oregon State University* (Corvallis, Oreg.: Oregon State University, 1992); Nancy L. Howard and Jacquelyn T. Rudolph, "Implementing TQM at Oregon State University," in *Quality and its Applications,* ed. J. F. L. Chan (New York: Penshaw Press, 1993), 315–20.

21. David Burda, "Hospital Employs TQM Principles to Rework its Evaluation System," *Modern Healthcare* 22 (August 1992): 60.

22. Nand Dureja, quality manager of Amdahl Australia, interview with author, June 1992; Nand Dureja, *Quality Improvement Process* (Melbourne, Australia: Amdahl Australia, 1991).

23. John Pederson, quality manager of BHP Steel and Transport, interview with author, June 1992; BHP Steel, *IDEAS: Idea Development Employees Award Scheme* (Melbourne, Australia: BHP Steel, 1992).

24. Ross L. Chapman, Paul Clarke, and Terry Sloan, "TQM in Continuous-Process Manufacturing: Dow-Corning (Australia) Pty Ltd," *International Journal of Quality and Reliability Management* 8 (October 1991): 77–90.

25. Patrick Dawson and Margaret Patrickson, "Total Quality Management in the Australian Banking Industry," *International Journal of Quality and Reliability* 8 (October 1991): 66–76.

26. Doug Rutherford, quality manager at Ford of Australia, interview with author, May 1992.

27. Carole A. Shifrin and Michael Mecham, "TQM Allows European Aerospace Firms to Devote New Attention to Quality," *Aviation Week & Space Technology* 135 (9 December 1991): 66.

28. Ibid.

29. Kaoru Ishikawa and David J. Lu, *What is Total Quality Control? The Japanese Way* (Englewood Cliffs, N.J.: Prentice Hall, 1985).

30. Toshiharu Koguri, "Providing Incentives to the QC Circle through an Evaluation System," in *Japan Quality Control Circles* (Tokyo: Asian Productivity Organization, 1983), 167–72.

Chapter 5

Performance Evaluation and the Reward and Recognition Process

Merit rating rewards people that do well in the system. It does not reward attempts to improve the system.
— W. Edwards Deming, *Out of the Crisis*

Performance appraisal is one of the most important things managers can do, but hardly anyone does it well. The system gets tied up in merit increases rather than personal development.
— Philip B. Crosby, *Let's Talk Quality*

An effective reward and recognition system requires an effective performance evaluation system. To offer rewards and recognitions that employees perceive to be fair, equitable, contingent on good performance, and valued, the performance evaluation system must display several characteristics. It must be reliable, so that employees perceive that good performance consistently leads to reward (contingent and instrumental in motivational terms). It must be valid; that is, it measures the important behaviors (here supporting TQM). It must be acceptable to the user (in TQM terms, the internal customer). And, it must be practical; it has to work given the realistic constraints of the organization.

Deming was against traditional types of performance evaluation, such as MBO, because he believed that such instruments pit individuals against each other. Individuals compete for high ratings in order to gain raises and promotions. Such competition hinders cooperation and teamwork. Individuals follow their own goals to the detriment of the organizational goals of quality improvement. For example, Deming was against MBO because it fosters competition to meet or exceed objectives.[1] Although there is employee participation in setting objectives, most objectives are in a quantitative form and, thus, define performance as productivity rather than as quality improvement.

Deming would probably eliminate most current evaluation systems. Unfortunately, that is not realistic for many organizations, which need some type of evaluation for promotion and personal development functions. Performance evaluation also is one of many organizational means of identifying training needs, customer needs, and supplying data for diagnoses of organizational processes. Thus, many organizations are grappling with the dilemma of how to evaluate performance within a TQM framework. Performance evaluation is the most significant area of conflict between current management practice and TQM principles.[2]

COMPONENTS OF A PERFORMANCE EVALUATION SYSTEM SUPPORTING TQM

An effective performance evaluation system under TQM would emphasize three areas for evaluation—the individual employee, the quality team, and the manager. Each level has performance criteria that can be evaluated by several types of evaluators. Performance criteria in turn can suggest various types of awards for the reward and recognition process (see Table 5.1).

The Individual Employee

Given our Western focus on the individual and our long organizational history of individual evaluation, we will most likely still have appraisal of individual employees. Instead of evaluating meeting performance goals—like sales quotas, productivity quotas, or number of customers served—the evaluation system should focus on performance supportive of TQM.

Criteria to Evaluate
- *Job skill development.* Job skills contribute to direct work activity, contribute to individual career development, and provide expertise that can be contributed to quality teams.
- *TQM skill development.* The employee should be evaluated on how well he or she is acquiring TQM skills through organizational training and self-education efforts.[3] Not only does the employee get feedback on skill development progress, but the

TABLE 5.1. Performance evaluation under TQM.

Focus	Criteria to evaluate	Purposes for evaluation	Evaluators	Possible bonuses/ awards
Individual employee	Job and TQM skill development, contribution to quality teams	Personal feedback, skill training needs, work assignments	Self, peers, supervisors	TQM skill attainment, team contribution
Quality team	Teamwork, TQM efforts, customer satisfaction	Team training needs, team diagnostics, customer needs	Team members, other teams, middle managers, external customers	Teamwork, problem solving, customer satisfaction
Manager	TQM leadership, customer satisfaction	Personal feedback, TQM culture diagnostics, leader training needs, customer needs	Self, peers, teams, external customers	Leadership, customer satisfaction

organization can use these data for programming TQM skill-training efforts.

- *Contribution to quality teams.* The employee should be evaluated on what he or she is contributing to the team. This could involve the degree of cooperation as well as what roles the employee takes on in the team effort—task-oriented roles (contributor, information seeker, synthesizer) and relations-oriented roles (harmonizer, encourager, expediter, leader).[4] The organization can use these data for team skills training and for work assignments to develop individuals' team skills.

Purposes for Evaluation

Evaluation can provide personal feedback to the employee on his or her progress as well as information to the organization on training needs and information to the supervisor on appropriate work assignments for the employee.

Evaluators

- *Self-evaluation.* The evaluation process can begin with the employee making a self-evaluation of his or her skill development and team contributions.[5]

- *Peers.* Peer evaluation can be reliable and valid, if there is frequent interaction with the individual.[6] Peers who work closely with the employee, particularly in quality teams, can evaluate interpersonal performance, such as contributions to teams.[7]

- *Supervisor.* The supervisor is the traditional evaluator in most performance evaluation systems. He or she is familiar with the employee's work and, at the same time, sees how the employee's efforts fit into the larger organizational plan. In traditional systems, however, the supervisor may take on the role of judge and even punishment dispenser. In performance evaluation under TQM the supervisor serves as a coach and advisor.[8]

Possible Awards

- *TQM skills attainment.* Individuals could receive a certificate for each level of TQM skills attainment reached (for example, various statistical tools learned) either through organizational training or self-improvement.

- *Team contribution.* Individuals could receive an award for overall contribution to team performance or for performance in some team role, such as facilitator or expediter.

The Quality Team

TQM efforts are centered around quality teams that monitor and improve important processes in the organization. The performance evaluation system must include data on team performance.[9]

Criteria to Evaluate

- *Teamwork.* The team should be evaluated on how well its members work together. These data can help the organization to program team-building training.

- *Team efforts in TQM.* Teams can be evaluated on how well they are performing in relation to other teams and the overall TQM effort. Again, this is basically a diagnostic evaluation for improving team performance.

- *Customer satisfaction.* Teams interact with both internal and external customers. Customer satisfaction can be measured in terms of promptness of service (for example, wait times), resolution of problems, and follow-up on service.

Purposes for Evaluation

Evaluation provides teams with information on their training needs and how well their team is operating. In addition, evaluation provides information on how well teams are serving customers.

Evaluators

- *Team members.* Members of the team can evaluate how well the team members work together, what roles are effective, and what further training is necessary.

- *Other teams.* Because teams need to work closely with other teams, these teams can evaluate teamwork within the team and cooperation with other teams.

- *Middle managers.* Middle managers are in a position to see how various team efforts are fitting into the overall TQM effort. Several middle managers could evaluate team efforts and contribution to overall quality improvement of the organization.

- *External customers.* Some teams interact directly with external customers who can evaluate service and problem solving.

Possible Awards

- *Teamwork.* Teams could be nominated by managers or other teams for teamwork awards that indicate the degree of cohesiveness and smooth working of a team. In addition, teams could be nominated by other teams who as internal customers were well served by particular teams.

- *Problem solving.* Teams could receive awards for solving particularly difficult quality problems or for innovative approaches to solving problems.

- *Customer satisfaction.* Both internal and external customers could nominate teams for particularly good customer service.

The Manager

Just as there will most likely be individual employee evaluation, manager evaluation also will occur.

Criteria to Evaluate

- *TQM leadership.* Leadership is one of Deming's principles.[10] Managers should be evaluated on their leadership in innovation, facilitating teams, removing performance obstacles, breaking down performance barriers, linking teams more directly to customer needs, and changing the corporate culture toward continuous quality improvement.[11] In other words, managers should provide the correct environment for TQM to operate effectively. These data can help the organization measure how well its corporate culture is moving toward TQM. In addition, these data can show what types of leadership training, such as facilitator training, are needed.

- *Customer satisfaction.* The quality of the organizational products or services is ultimately defined by customer demands, so it is logical that managers should be evaluated on measures of customer satisfaction: overall satisfaction, service delivery, accuracy, and quality.

Purposes for Evaluation

Evaluation provides managers personal feedback on how well they are meeting their quality goals. The organization benefits by receiving information about how well its leadership is transforming the existing culture to a quality culture, the training needs of its leaders, and how well leaders are serving customers.

Evaluators

- *Self-evaluation.* Managers can begin their evaluation process by evaluating their own contributions to the overall TQM effort.
- *Peers.* At the manager level, peers are many times internal customers. Thus, peers can evaluate management contributions as well as performance toward satisfying internal customers.
- *Teams.* Quality teams can evaluate how managers facilitate team performance—how they provide needed resources, coordinate various team efforts, and implement team solutions to quality problems.
- *External customers.* Several organizations are evaluating their managers according to customer responses to surveys.[12]

Possible Awards

- *Leadership.* Managers could receive awards for leadership of the TQM effort—facilitating team efforts, inspiring through role modeling, innovative leadership decisions, bringing customers and quality teams closer together.

- *Customer satisfaction.* Customers could nominate managers who either provide excellent personal service or whose departments continually provide excellent team service. In addition, special attention to customer needs could be an award category.

PRINCIPLES FOR IMPROVING PERFORMANCE EVALUATION UNDER TQM

Effective performance evaluation must support, not hinder, TQM efforts. Several principles follow that should be a part of any effective performance evaluation system under TQM.[13]

Use performance evaluation to reflect the mission of the organization toward continuous quality improvement. Traditional performance evaluation focuses on meeting productivity goals and on meeting or bettering past performance. Performance evaluation under TQM should appraise how individuals and teams are improving organizational processes.

Link performance evaluation to training. Training and education comprise two of Deming's 14 principles.[14] A primary function of performance evaluation under TQM is to identify developmental needs of individuals and teams. Thus, performance evaluation should lead the training process by identifying training needs and objectives to be met in training.

Use performance evaluation to provide feedback on TQM efforts. From chapter 3, we saw that feedback on performance is required by several motivational theories. Effective feedback requires an open communication system that crosses organizational barriers and allows constructive information to be exchanged.

Evaluate performance from multiple perspectives. Different evaluators see performance from different perspectives. Thus, multiple evaluators can provide more information on the factors that influence performance.[15] Comparing the input of the various evaluators can show where significant disagreements occur. Such disagreements can occur because one group of evaluators, such as managers, is focusing too much on personal causes of performance and is ignoring important system causes.[16] Multiple evaluators thus move the focus of performance to system factors or to the external attributions identified in chapter 6.

Use performance appraisals to focus on barriers to individual improvement. As stated in chapter 6, performance evaluation should move away from its traditional emphasis on placing blame on individuals for poor performance. Instead, the emphasis should be placed on removing system barriers to better performance, such as lack of training or lack of the appropriate tools or problems in coordination.[17]

Reduce employee evaluation apprehension through effective feedback in appraisal sessions. The performance evaluation literature provides several good recommendations for reducing employees' apprehension and defensiveness about having their performance critiqued in appraisal sessions.[18]

1. *Focus the discussion on performance, not personality.* Employees can change performance, but they cannot change too much about their personality.

2. *Try to differentiate personnel matters from personal development.* Separate information about raises and promotions from the discussion of ways to improve employee skills and contributions.

3. *Actively listen to the employee.* Hear what employees are telling you. They are providing valuable information not only about how they perceive the situation but also about aspects of the work situation of which you may be unaware.

4. *Focus on supportive comments.* Research shows that supportive comments increase employee satisfaction with the appraisal session, while criticism leads to less improvement.

A PUBLIC SECTOR PERFORMANCE EVALUATION EXAMPLE: THE TEAM-ORIENTED PERFORMANCE MANAGEMENT PROJECT

The U.S. Navy, like a number of federal government organizations, has directed that its version of TQM, called *total quality leadership* (TQL), be implemented throughout the fleet. (The Navy prefers the term *leadership* to *management* because it believes that leadership is a more active concept than management.) On the one hand, the Navy, with its long history of sailing traditions and its unique command structure (the captain of a ship is almost an absolute ruler), is perhaps the most conservative of the military services. On the other hand, much of the early federal government work on TQM was done by the Navy through its Navy Personnel R & D Center (NPRDC).[19]

Continuing in its vanguard role in TQL, NPRDC is carrying out a five-year project on performance evaluation called *team-oriented performance management* (TOPM).[20] Performance evaluation in the federal government is unique because by law federal employees must be evaluated once a year on an individual basis. Thus, until the law is changed, Deming's desire to eliminate individual evaluation is not possible at the federal level. Consequently, the Navy directed NPRDC to create a system to try to accommodate TQM principles within the constraints of the rules on federal performance appraisal.

TOPM has three components. The first is measurement of the process. TOPM is decentralized. Each Navy organization develops its own version of TOPM within the overall guidelines. For a given unit, the TQM steering committee identifies those working in the process and their customers. A TOPM team then identifies measures of performance in the process for the purposes of gauging progress. Typical measures are customer satisfaction data, product quality, and process quality data.

The second component is the appraisal of individuals and teams. Employees are evaluated on individual contributions to process improvement including team contributions and preparation for future process improvement (TQM skill development). Teams are evaluated on team process improvement. Evaluators are supervisors and peers.

The third component is productivity gain sharing. Individuals and teams can share in cost savings accrued from quality improvement efforts. The size of the award depends on the size of the increase and the value of the improvement. Gains are shared on a 50/50 basis between the employees and the organization.

CONCLUSIONS

Effective performance evaluation underlies any effective reward and recognition program. An effective performance evaluation system for TQM requires performance criteria that support the quality and customer orientation of the organization. Furthermore, such a system requires evaluative feedback from several sources—the individual employee, the quality team, management, and external customers. Finally, TQM performance evaluation supports not only the reward and recognition process but also provides data for performance feedback, for identifying training needs, for diagnosing team and organizational operations, and for identifying customer needs.

NOTES

1. W. Edwards Deming, *Out of the Crisis* (Cambridge, Mass.: MIT Center for Advanced Engineering Study, 1986), 102.

2. David E. Bowen and Edward E. Lawler, "Total Quality-Oriented Human Resources Management," *Organizational Dynamics* (spring 1992): 29–41.

3. Ibid.

4. The classic study of group roles is K. D. Benne and P. Sheats, "Functional Roles of Group Members," *Journal of Social Issues* 4 (1948): 41–49.

5. J. Bruce Prince, "Performance Appraisal and Reward Practices in Total Quality Organizations," *Quality Management Journal* 1, no. 2 (1994): 36–46.

6. Gary P. Latham and Kenneth N. Wexley, *Increasing Productivity through Performance Appraisal*, 2d ed. (Reading, Mass.: Addison Wesley, 1994).

7. Prince, "Performance Appraisal."

8. Dennis M. Daley, "Pay for Performance, Performance Appraisal, and Total Quality Management," *Public Productivity and Management Review* 16 (1992): 39–51.

9. Bowen and Lawler, "Total Quality-Oriented Human Resources Management;" Prince, "Performance Appraisal."

10. Deming, *Out of the Crisis*, 23.

11. Bruce J. Avolio, "The Alliance of Total Quality and the Full Range of Leadership," and D. A. Waldman, "Transformational Leadership in Multifunctional Teams," both in *Improving Organizational Effectiveness through Transformational Leadership*, ed. Bernard M. Bass and Bruce J. Avolio (Thousand Oaks, Calif.: Sage, 1993).

12. Patricia Keehley, "Does TQM Spell 'Time to Quit Merit'?" *Public Productivity and Management Review* 16 (1993): 387–94.

13. Barry R. Nathan, John Milliman, and Nida Backaitis, "The Deming Challenge to Performance Appraisal: Implications for Research and Practice" (paper presented at the annual meeting of the Society of Industrial and Organizational Psychology, St. Louis, Mo., April 1991).

14. Deming, *Out of the Crisis*, 23.

15. Prince, "Performance Appraisal."

16. Kenneth P. Carson, Robert L. Cardy, and Gregory H. Dobbins, "Upgrade the Employee Evaluation Process," *HR Magazine* (November 1992): 88–92; Prince, "Performance Appraisal."

17. Carson, Cardy, and Dobbins, "Upgrade the Employee Evaluation Process."

18. Latham and Wexley, *Increasing Productivity through Performance Appraisal.*

19. Mary Walton, *Deming Management at Work* (New York: Putnam, 1990), 147–84.

20. Delbert Nebeker and Michael White, "Team-Oriented Performance Management," concept paper, Navy Personnel Research and Development Center, San Diego, Calif., 1990.

Part II

Special Issues in Reward and Recognition

Chapter 6

An Attribution Theory Approach to the Reward and Recognition Process

Supervisors commonly make the mistake of overadjustment when they direct to the attention of one of their people any mistake or defect, without first ascertaining that the worker was actually responsible for the mistake. Did the worker make the mistake, or was the system responsible for it?
—W. Edwards Deming, *Out of the Crisis*

There has been surprisingly little application of psychological theories toward explaining how human behavior operates in a TQM organization. In chapter 3 we looked at how principles from various motivation theories may be applied to TQM. Here we look at another perspective, attribution theory, that may have implications for interpersonal relations between supervisors and employees in a TQM organization.[1]

ATTRIBUTION THEORY

Attribution theory is based on the assumption that human beings as rational beings attempt to explain the causes of behavior in themselves and others. They tend to employ two types of explanations or attributions—internal (sometimes called *personal* or *dispositional)* attributions, which infer that behavior is caused by internal factors, such as effort, personality, motivation, ability, and experience, and external (also called *situational)* attributions, which infer that behavior is caused by external factors, such as task difficulty, organizational influences, or even luck.[2]

97

Stability Dimension

These two attribution factors can be further divided along a stability dimension.[3] On the one side, stable internal attributions, would be perceived as relatively permanent traits, such as individual skill, personality, and experience, while unstable internal attributions, such as individual effort and motivation, would continually change. Stable external attributions would be relatively permanent environmental attributes, such as task difficulty or organizational procedures, while unstable external attributions would be seemingly random factors, such as luck.

Criteria for Making Attributions

How does an individual make either an internal or external attribution? There are three criteria for choosing which attribution is appropriate.[4]

1. *Distinctiveness.* Distinctiveness is the degree to which the individual whose behavior is being observed responds differently to different (distinctive) tasks. If the individual responds similarly to different tasks, the observer makes an internal attribution (that is, something inside the individual is causing similar responses to different tasks). If the individual responds differently to different tasks, the observer makes an external attribution (that is, different task situations outside of the individual cause different behaviors). For example, if I see an employee do well on one task situation and poorly on another, I assume the performance was caused by the differences in the task, such as task complexity or task difficulty (external attribution). On the other hand, if the employee does well on a number of different tasks, I assume it must be something inside the employee, such as personality or motivation or ability (internal attribution).

2. *Consistency.* Consistency refers to the degree to which the individual's behavior varies over time. If the individual responds consistently over time in different situations, the observer makes an internal attribution (that is, the individual's ability or personality is causing consistent behavior over time). If the individual responds differently over time in the same situation,

the observer makes an external attribution (that is, characteristics of this particular situation are causing the behavior in the individual).

3. *Consensus.* Consensus is the degree to which others respond to a task in the same manner. If others respond similarly, the observer makes an external attribution (that is, the characteristics of the task, such as its difficulty, are causing everyone to respond poorly). If others respond differently, the observer makes an internal attribution (that is, internal differences in ability and personality among the various individuals are causing different behaviors on this task). For example, if everybody has difficulty with a new computer program, you conclude that it's something about the program, such as poor instructions or confusing menus, that is causing the poor performance (external attribution). On the other hand, if some people do well and some poorly on the task, you conclude it must be something inside these individuals, such as different individual levels of prior ability with computers, causing the differences in performance (internal attribution).

To summarize the effects of the three criteria, a person makes an internal attribution about behavior he or she sees when distinctiveness of the situation is low (the person performing the behavior exhibits the same behavior over different situations), consistency of behavior over different situations is high, and consensus is low (other people act differently in that situation). A person makes an external attribution when distinctiveness is high (the person in question acts differently in different situations), consistency is low (the person acts differently over time), and consensus is high (other people act the same in that situation).

Attribution Errors

People are subject to basic errors in making attributions.

Fundamental Attribution Error. The fundamental attribution error occurs when individuals default to an internal attribution in many situations; that is, they perceive that behavior is caused by personal factors a majority of the time.[5] This error is theorized by some to be an information processing error caused by lack of close attention to the task.[6] For example, there may be a lack of close observation of behavior which implies that the observer cannot see a range of causes including external causes. In other words, it is easier to see personal causes for most behavior than to try to search out all the different situations that may be causing a behavior.

To illustrate, a manager may only step into a particular employee's office for a few minutes once a week or so. In that short time the manager sees little of the workings of the many organizational factors that influence the employee's work. It is impossible for the manager to see how organizational training, help from others, various types of equipment, and departmental procedures directly affect that employee's work in such a short time period. It is much simpler for the manager to take the easy way out and conclude that any good results he or she sees from the employee are caused by that employee's motivation and any poor results are caused by lack of motivation.

Self-Serving Bias.   A second error, the self-serving bias, occurs when people, in order to protect their own self-esteem, will tend to make internal attributions about their own successful behavior and external attributions about their own unsuccessful behavior; that is, success is due to my own hard work, but failure is not my fault.[7] A study of CEO communications to the public and to their stockholders nicely illustrates this self-serving bias. The CEOs took personal credit for increases in growth and profitability in their companies in good years. But in bad years they explained poor performance as due to factors outside of their control, such as a sluggish economy.[8]

Applications of Attribution Theory to Organization Behavior

Attribution theory has broad application to organizational behavior. Attribution frameworks have been proposed for employment selection, achievement motivation, leadership, and even writing letters of recommendation.[9]

ATTRIBUTION THEORY AND TQM

There are a number of implications for using attribution theory to explain human performance in the TQM organization. First we will look at how attribution concepts fit with Deming's ideas. Then we will look at applications to two important areas—performance evaluation and leadership.

Attributions and Deming

Deming advocated reducing performance variability in the organization through continuous quality improvement.[10] He advocated getting control of wide swings in product and service quality and reliability through smoothing out variability in organizational processes. To do this, Deming emphasized that the causes of this variability must be identified and controlled. He concentrated on two causes: common or system causes (materials, equipment, procedures, and training) and special causes (random variations due to individual events). As shown in Table 6.1, Deming's common causes (system variables) would be similar to stable external attribution factors in attribution theory. His special causes would be unstable external attribution factors (for example, the random occurrence, or you might say the bad luck, of a particular machine breaking down on a particular day). In fact, Deming's mentor, Shewhart, who invented SPC charts, originally termed special causes *chance factors,*[11] which is very similar to the unstable external attribution of luck. In addition, unstable internal attribution factors may play a role (for example, an employee working poorly because he or she does not feel well that day).

Attribution of Performance and the Reward and Recognition Process

An attribution theory approach can be helpful here in explaining how supervisors traditionally approach the reward and recognition process. The key is how they attribute the performance on which the reward or award is based. If a supervisor sees good performance and attributes it to internal factors within the individual (motivation and ability), he or she may believe that the individual is working hard and confer a reward or recognition. If, on the other hand, the supervisor sees good performance and attributes it to external factors (an easy task, help from others), he or she may believe that the person is less deserving of a reward or recognition (see Figure 6.1).

In the case of poor performance, an internal attribution (the performance was due to lack of motivation or ability and thus was the employee's fault) may result in some punishment applied to the employee,

TABLE 6.1. Relation of attribution theory to Deming's causes of variability and traditional and TQM organizational responses.

Attribution	Example	Traditional organizational response		Deming cause	TQM organizational response	
		Poor performance	Good performance		Poor performance	Good performance
Internal						
Stable	Personality	Punish individual	Reward individual	Special	Match personality styles to team roles, leadership role models	Reward role taking in teams, reward role modeling
Stable	Ability	Punish individual	Reward individual	Common	Skills training	Reward skills development
Unstable	Motivation	Punish individual	Reward individual	Special	Team help, leadership inspiration	Reward contribution to teams
External						
Stable	Procedures, resources, equipment	Corrective action	Less likely to reward individual	Common	Improve organizational factors	Reward team contributions to process improvements
Unstable	Luck, random variation	Corrective action	Less likely to reward individual	Special	Monitor special causes	

Observation	Evaluation	Attribution	Response
Observe → employee behaviors	Apply → attribution criteria • Distinctiveness • Consistency • Consensus	Make internal → attribution to • Personality • Motivation *if* Employee reacts the same to dfferent situations; others react differently to the same situatation • Low distinctiveness • High consistency • Low consensus	Reward good behavior *and* Punish poor behavior
	→	Make external → attribution to • Training • Procedures • Other system factors *if* Employee reacts differently to different situations; others react the same to the same situation • High distinctiveness • Low consistency • High consensus	Less apt to reward good behavior *and* More apt to fix system factors for poor behavior

FIGURE 6.1.   An attribution theory model of management's response to employee behavior.

while an external attribution (it's outside of his or her control, so it is not the employee's fault) may result in a corrective action to the system factors that caused the problem.[12]

A study of nursing supervisors supports these ideas. The supervisors were given brief accounts of errors of nursing staff. When the supervisors received information that the errors were linked to internal causes (lack of motivation or ability), they indicated that they would more likely to respond directly to the nurses (try to better motivate or train them). Conversely, when the supervisors received information focusing on external causes (over-demanding work schedules), they were more apt to take corrective action toward the situation (reschedule the work more efficiently).[13]

Performance Evaluation

Dealing with the Fundamental Attribution Error.   Deming's major complaint against traditional performance appraisal was that supervisors rate individuals on system performance that they cannot control or change by working harder.[14] This is a restatement of the fundamental attribution error—overestimating the influence of internal factors while underestimating the effects of external factors.

Recent research supports this fundamental attribution error from a TQM perspective. An experimental study showed that raters assigned responsibility for work performance largely to the employee even in the face of system factors. In other words, they continued to focus on personal factors even when system factors were dominant.[15] Raters tended to default to evaluating internal factors in others, because this was easier to handle than trying to deal with the many effects of system factors on employee performance.

A similar study showed further evidence of the fundamental attribution error in performance appraisal. Managers made fewer external attributions when evaluating other employees' performance than they did in evaluating their own performance. This was because managers knew their own performance better than the performance of others. Obviously the managers saw their own performance on a continuous basis, while they saw the performance of others less often. Thus, with all these data on themselves, the managers could readily see the influence of external factors, such as organizational procedures and the cooperation of others, on their own performance. For others, however, they had less data and were less aware of the influence of external factors on others' performance. They thus defaulted to the fundamental attribution error.[16]

Attributional explorations of performance evaluation have provided some clues on how to reduce the fundamental attribution error. For example, explanations of the fundamental attribution error in the manager–employee evaluation situation focus on factors in the information exchange process between the manager and the employee. Managers tend to emphasize internal attributions of employee performance for several reasons. First, important decisions, such as individual promotions and raises, require internal attributional information (for example, managers believe that promotions and raises should be given to motivated employees). Second, managers tend to have a high internal locus of control (they believe that they have control over their lives) and thus naturally focus on internal factors. Third, managers tend to develop personal relationships with employees and focus on personal rather than task factors in performance evaluation.[17]

On the other hand, there are factors that can reduce the emphasis on internal attribution. For example, in a study where managers actively interacted with employees in the performance appraisal process, more specific job-related information was exchanged, which caused an attributional shift toward leniency for both high and low employee performance. In other words, managers attributed less internal responsibility for performance and less punitive comments after active information exchange with their employees.[18] Indeed, Deming stressed that management must involve employees in continually collecting data on performance processes in order to understand employee performance and thereby improve performance by focusing on the correct causes.[19]

Transitioning from Self-Serving Bias to a Team Emphasis.   A second influence that has not been addressed directly in Deming's approach is the self-serving bias—individuals' desire to attribute success to themselves and failure to factors outside of them. What will be the effect when Deming principles begin to work in the organization? Following Deming's line of reasoning, success must be attributed to the team—not to any individual, no matter how much effort he or she has expended in making the system work. Organizations that have adopted Deming principles have dealt with this problem through a type of compromise— an emphasis on teamwork and team rewards, such as productivity gain sharing with the team, but also on individual rewards for facilitating the team effort.[20]

Another answer may lie in four of Deming's 14 principles— change the organizational culture, drive out fear, break down barriers, and improve the worker's pride in work.[21] When this transition has occurred in an organization, the focus will change from an emphasis on individual performance to an emphasis on organizational performance as the basic unit of analysis. Partial support for this contention was seen in the study where managers who openly and actively shared job information with employees in evaluating performance tended toward attributional leniency (that is, they placed less emphasis on internal responsibility for performance and were more knowledgeable about the effects of external factors).

Further, attribution researchers are beginning to focus on external organizational factors beyond the control of the performer that must be taken into account when evaluating performance. For example,

H. John Bernardin, a performance evaluation expert, identified 22 external factors as potential constraints on performance to be evaluated, such as inadequate performance of supervisors, unpredictable work loads, and lack of proper equipment. Bernardin advocates an organizational training program for identifying legitimate external factors and building a strategy for reducing these factors.[22] Although Bernardin is approaching the problem from an independent direction, his idea is surprisingly close to Deming's principle that common causes in the system must be identified and controlled in order to reduce performance variability and thus improve quality.

Consequently, if the organization successfully makes the transition from emphasizing individual performance to emphasizing group performance, then the individual should truly see him- or herself as a team member; he or she will define his or her self-image in terms of the team. Evidence from self-concept theory shows that an emphasis on team performance closely relates to an individual's self-image becoming more closely aligned with the team.[23] Further, evidence from group dynamics research shows that positive team performance strongly relates to the identification with a team image by the individual team members.[24]

Theoretically, we can see how this happens through the value change model in psychology. According to this model, individuals acquire values through three successively more involving influence processes. First is the weak process where individuals merely display these values in public in superficial compliance with organization pressures (for example, "I'll exhibit these values only when someone in the organization demands it"). Second is the stronger process of identification where employees role model the values of dynamic organization leaders (for example, "I'll demonstrate these values because I respect and want to be like the leader"). Third is the strongest process of internalization where individuals acquire organization values because they personally relate to these values and therefore want to merge them permanently with their own values (for example, "I believe in the organizational values strongly enough that they have become my own values").[25] If the organizational culture is sufficiently changed toward TQM so that the individual feels an integral part of the culture and wants to define his or her work success as a member of this organization, the deepest level of value change—internalization—has occurred; that is, the organizational values have become a permanent part of the individual's self-concept.

If such internalization has occurred, personal (that is, internal) attributions will be refocused. Instead of success being perceived as an individual accomplishment, the attribution will now become the perception of success due to oneself as an integral part of the team. The former internal attribution factors of individual ability and effort will now be seen as the team's collective ability and effort (group efficacy).[26]

Leadership and Attribution Theory

One of the many applications of attribution theory to organizational behavior is in the area of leadership. Not surprisingly, leadership underlies several of Deming's 14 principles.[27] The attribution theory of leadership states that managers respond to employees in a two-stage process. In the first stage, managers make an internal or external attribution about an employee's performance based on the three attributional criteria of distinctiveness, consistency, and consensus. In the second stage, managers respond to the employee's performance based on the attribution they have formulated.[28] If the manager perceives that good performance is internally caused, individual merit raises are given. If the manager perceives that good performance is externally caused, group rewards are given.

Attribution theory would be particularly relevant for quality improvement from the perspective of how managers diagnose and respond to the problem of poor employee performance. Traditionally, when a manager observed poor (or substandard) employee performance, he or she would focus on an internal attribution and believe that the poor performance was due to lack of motivation. The manager would then respond by monitoring the employee more closely and manipulating individual incentives or even administering punishments, such as reprimands or reductions in pay. Deming would view this manager as trying to improve the process by responding ineffectively to special causes.[29]

On the other hand, in the TQM organization the manager would focus on the attributional criteria of distinctiveness (how does this employee react to factors in different task situations?) and consensus (how do other employees, particularly team members, react in a given task situation?). In this case, the TQM manager would be more apt to make an external attribution and believe that the employee's poor performance was caused by poor equipment, inappropriate work load, unrealistic deadlines, organizational obstacles, insufficient information, and inadequate resources. The manager then would respond by trying to change the work situation: install better equipment, change the work load, create realistic deadlines, remove organizational obstacles, supply correct information, and provide adequate resources. Deming, in turn, would view this manager as improving the process by correctly responding to organizational system causes.

It would appear that an attributional theory of leadership focusing on external attributional processes would be the correct approach to implementing Deming's principle of leadership. There is a problem, however, in that the manager may make a correct internal attribution that a part of the poor performance was due to the individual employee's lack of ability. The appropriate managerial response to lack of ability is skills training, which also happens to be another of Deming's principles.[30] How, then, does Deming's training principle fit into the general approach proposed here that the manager should evaluate and then respond to employee performance from an external attributional-systems causes perspective?

The answer may lie in the stability dimension of attribution theory as shown in Table 6.1. The system causes emphasized here (for example, organizational obstacles, information flow, and resources) are stable external causes in terms of attribution theory. On the other hand, the employee ability problem is a stable internal attribution. Therefore, if we are to use attribution theory as a theoretical underpinning of Deming's principles, we may eventually see evolution of managerial thought in TQM away from a strict emphasis on only system causes underlying performance problems (stable external attributions) and toward a broader emphasis on stable causes (stable external system causes *and* stable internal causes) that can be corrected by TQM organizational practices, such as leadership and training, that simultaneously address both types of causes.

IMPLICATIONS FOR THE REWARD AND RECOGNITION PROCESS

How Attributions Change as Organizations Implement TQM

1. *Eventually in the TQM organization there will be less emphasis on individual worker responsibility for performance (internal attributions) and more emphasis on team responsibility.* At present in developing TQM organizations there is still a tendency toward evaluating internal attributions for performance and conferring

individual rewards for individual effort. Some TQM organizations have gone further and have dual performance evaluations where person and system factors are jointly analyzed. In these organizations, managers have a better understanding of how system factors influence performance.[31] As TQM becomes fully integrated into the organizational culture, there will be a transition from individual evaluation toward team evaluation and conferring team rewards and recognition.

2. *Eventually in the TQM organization supervisors will see poor performance less in terms of individual blame (internal attribution) and more in terms of problematic system causes (external attribution).* There will be less emphasis on punishing individuals for performance that is largely out of their control. There will be more emphasis on corrective action aimed at system causes (acquiring better-quality materials from TQM-oriented vendors, maintaining equipment more efficiently, improving procedures, and providing extensive training).

3. *Eventually in the TQM organization employees will focus less on internal attributions of performance and will focus more on team influences on performance.* Rewards and recognition will be defined less in terms of individual employee preferences and more in terms of team preferences.

Attributional Applications for Reaching the Fully Integrated TQM Organization

1. *Create more open communication between management and workers.* Attribution research has shown that a greater exchange of job-related information between supervisors and employees produces less emphasis on internal responsibility for performance. At the same time a greater focus on external causes ensues.

2. *Create performance evaluation systems focused on external causes.* The organization should move away from evaluation systems that emphasize and reward individual responsibility for events, and institute an evaluation system that focuses on identifying and controlling external factors (common causes) of performance through team efforts at quality improvement.

3. *Emphasize leader styles that have an external attribution perspective.* The organization needs to train its leaders to take an external attributional perspective in which managers diagnose

performance problems in terms of external (system) causes and respond to these problems by attempting to change aspects of the situation (remove obstacles, improve resources, and provide better information). Moreover, managers should dispense rewards and recognition for team efforts focused on correcting these external causes.

CONCLUSIONS

Attribution theory can help both researchers and practitioners understand the psychological dynamics underlying the corporate cultural change occurring in a TQM organization. Attribution theory can provide a theoretical framework that allows researchers to test how values, attitudes, perceptions, and resulting behaviors change under TQM. Moreover, attribution theory provides a link between the psychology of interpersonal perceptions and Deming's views of special and system causes. Finally, attribution theory provides a means for practitioners to understand how performance evaluation, distributing rewards and awards, leadership, and value change fit together in a TQM corporate culture.

NOTES

1. Stephen B. Knouse and Michael White, "An Attribution Theory Approach to Deming's Deadly Disease of Performance Appraisal," in *Proceedings of the International Academy of Business Disciplines* (New Orleans, La.: 1993): 335–42.

2. A good summary of attribution theory occurs in Gifford Weary, Michael A. Stanley, and John H. Harvey, *Attribution* (New York: Springer-Verlag, 1989).

3. Bernard Weiner, Irene H. Frieze, A. Kukla, A. L. Reed, S. Rest, and R. M. Rosenbaum, *Perceiving the Causes of Success and Failure* (Morristown, N.J.: General Learning Press, 1971).

4. Weary, Stanley, and Harvey, *Attribution*.

5. Larry Ross, "The Intuitive Psychologist and His Shortcomings: Distortions in the Attribution Process," in *Advances in Experimental Social Psychology*, vol. 10, ed. Leonard Berkowitz (New York: Academic Press, 1977): 173–220.

6. Weary, Stanley, and Harvey, *Attribution*.

7. Ibid.

8. Gerald R. Salancik and James R. Meindl, "Corporate Attributions as Strategic Illusions of Management Control," *Administrative Science Quarterly* 29 (1984): 238–54.

9. Stephen B. Knouse, "The Role of Attribution Theory in Personnel Employment Selection: A Review of the Recent Literature," *Journal of General Psychology* 116 (1989): 183–96; C. Ward Struthers, Nina L. Colwill, and Raymond P. Perry, "An Attributional Analysis of Decision Making in a Personnel Selection Interview," *Journal of Applied Social Psychology* 22 (1992): 801–18; Bernard Weiner, "An Attributional Theory of Achievement Motivation," *Psychological Bulletin* 92 (1985): 548–73; Stephen G. Green and Terence R. Mitchell, "Attributional Processes of Leaders in Leader-Member Interactions," *Organizational Behavior and Human Performance* 23 (1979): 429–58; Stephen B. Knouse, "An Attributional Theory Approach to the Letter of Recommendation," *International Journal of Management* 4 (1987): 5–13; Stephen B. Knouse, "The Letter of Recommendation: Writer Familiarity with the Recommendee," *Management Communication Quarterly* 2 (1988): 46–62.

10. W. Edwards Deming, *Out of the Crisis* (Cambridge, Mass.: MIT Center for Advanced Engineering Study, 1986), 318.

11. Walter A. Shewhart, *Economic Control of Quality of Manufactured Product* (New York: Van Nostrand, 1931).

12. Kenneth P. Carson, Robert L. Cardy, and Gregory H. Dobbins, "Upgrade the Employee Evaluation Process," *HRMagazine* (November 1992): 88–92.

13. Terence R. Mitchell and Robert E. Wood, "Supervisors' Responses to Subordinate Poor Performance: A Test of an Attribution Model," *Organizational Behavior and Human Performance* 25 (1980): 123–38.

14. Deming, *Out of the Crisis,* 109.

15. Kenneth P. Carson, Robert L. Cardy, and Gregory H. Dobbins, "Performance Appraisal as Effective Management or Deadly Management Disease," *Group and Organization Studies* 16 (1991): 143–59.

16. Scott L. Martin and Richard J. Klimoski, "Use of Verbal Protocols to Trace Cognitions Associated with Self- and Supervisor Evaluations of Performance," *Organizational Performance and Human Decision Processes* 46 (1990): 135–54.

17. Robert L. Heneman, David B. Greenberger, and Chigozie A. Anonyuo, "Attributions and Exchanges: The Effects of Interpersonal Factors on the Diagnosis of Employee Performance," *Academy of Management Journal* 32 (1989): 466–76.

18. Dennis A. Gioia and Henry P. Sims, "Cognition–Behavior Connections: Attribution and Verbal Behavior in Leader-Subordinate Interac-

tions," *Organizational Behavior and Human Decision Processes* 37 (1986): 197–229.

19. Deming, *Out of the Crisis,* 371.

20. Mary Walton, *The Deming Management Method* (New York: Putnam, 1986); Joyce Ward and Vel Hulton, *Total Quality Management Case Studies: 1988 Recipients of the Malcolm Baldrige National Quality Award* (San Diego, Calif.: Navy Personnel Research and Development Center, 1990).

21. Deming, *Out of the Crisis,* 23–24.

22. H. John Bernardin, "Increasing the Accuracy of Performance Measurement: A Proposed Solution to Erroneous Attributions," *Human Resource Planning* 12 (1989): 239–50.

23. Erving Goffman, *The Presentation of Self in Everyday Life* (Garden City, N.Y.: Doubleday, 1959).

24. Daniel C. Feldman, "The Development and Enforcement of Group Norms," *Academy of Management Review* 9 (1984): 47–53.

25. Herbert Kelman, "Compliance, Identification, and Internalization: Three Processes of Attitude Change," *Journal of Conflict Resolution* 2 (1959): 251–60.

26. Kristina Whitney, "Improving Group Task Performance: The Role of Group Goals and Group Efficacy," *Human Performance* 7 (1994): 55–78.

27. Deming, *Out of the Crisis,* 23–24.

28. Terence R. Mitchell, Stephen C. Green, and Robert E. Wood, "An Attribution Model of Leadership and the Poor Performing Subordinate," in *Research in Organizational Behavior,* vol. 3, ed. Barry Staw and Larry L. Cummings (Greenwich, Conn.: JAI Press, 1981); Gary Yukl, "Managerial Leadership: A Review of Theory and Research," *Journal of Management* 15 (1989): 251–89.

29. Deming, *Out of the Crisis,* 314.

30. Ibid., 52.

31. Carson, Cardy, and Dobbins, "Upgrade the Employee Evaluation Process."

Chapter 7

Emerging Issues in Reward and Recognition

Principle 7: Institute leadership. . . . The required transforma-
tion of Western style of management requires that managers be
leaders.
         —W. Edwards Deming, *Out of the Crisis*

TQM requires leaders . . . The developing research about leaders
suggests that they have a long-term perspective, that they are
visionaries with Merlin-like powers.
         —Edward Fuchs, "Future Issues in
         Total Quality Management"

The contest and the measurement are the key. The prize is not
significant, it only matters that all of an individual's contem-
poraries know that he or she has fought the good fight and won.
         —Philip B. Crosby, *Quality Is Free*

There are several issues that are currently coming to the forefront and
will be of significant impact in the future for the reward and recognition process.

THE ROLE OF CHARISMATIC LEADERSHIP

Leadership is one of Deming's principles. *Leadership* is defined as the
process of influencing others toward meeting organizational goals.[1]
There are a number of leadership theories available that are similar to
the theories of motivation described in chapter 3 that we can draw on
to understand how leaders will manage the TQM organization. One
approach is an attributional theory of leadership, which was covered

in chapter 6. Another theory currently receiving a lot of attention, both by researchers and by practicing managers, is charisma, which we shall address now.

Transactional versus Transformational Leaders

According to this approach, there are basically two types of leaders. Transactional leaders manage employees. They recognize what individual employees want, clarify what needs to be done, and help employees accomplish their goals. In a sense, they are good practitioners of reinforcement theory and expectancy theory, described in chapter 3.[2]

Transformational leaders, on the other hand, change the entire organization; they transform the organization toward their vision of what the organization should be doing and where it should be going.[3] The charismatic leader is one type of transformational leader.

Charismatic Leaders

Where do charismatic leaders come from? There is one group of researchers who believe that charisma, which means *gift* in Greek, is inherent in the individual. Charismatic leaders are born, not made. There is another larger camp, however, that holds the more prevalent belief that charismatic leadership is actually the unique relationship between the leader and the followers. Charisma is then a special set of behaviors that influences this relationship and produces unique reactions in the followers: (1) high levels of performance, (2) loyalty and devotion toward the leader, (3) enthusiasm for the leader and his or her ideas, and (4) subordinating individual interests toward meeting the organizational goals.[4]

How do charismatic leaders create such an intense following? They display several types of behaviors.

1. *Propose a vision.* Charismatic leaders have a strong sense of where they are going and where the organization should be going and can transmit this vision toward their followers so that the vision becomes a shared vision. In the TQM organization, this vision would include a transformation of the organization toward a total commitment to quality: customer focus, employee involvement, and business operations centered on quality improvement.[5]

2. *Propose a map for action.* Charismatic leaders are not only visionary, but know how to reach their dreams. They can effectively and clearly map out how to pursue the vision. They create a "master template" for action.[6] There are two facets of a vision to clarify: physical and behavioral. The physical side refers to what the organization will look like—its TQM structure, information flow, and physical environment. The behavioral side has to do with what will it feel like to work in the organization—management styles, interpersonal relations, and teamwork.

3. *Frame the vision.* Charismatics can frame the vision in a clear snapshot that links the vision to deeply held organizational values. Many times the leader will use metaphors and stories to reinforce this snapshot. Mary Kay Ash frequently uses the metaphor of the bumblebee: "A bee shouldn't be able to fly; its body is too heavy for its wings. But the bumblebee doesn't know this and it flies very well. . . . Women come to us not knowing they can fly. Finally, with help and encouragement, they find their wings. . . ."[7] Steven Jobs, when he was with Apple Computer, used the story of David and Goliath to compare his small company to the menacing giant IBM. These metaphors and stories are simple, are direct, and forcefully reinforce the organization's values. TQM organizations use similar metaphors, such as "walk the talk." Leaders' behaviors must match their exhortations.[8]

4. *Be willing to take risks.* Charismatic leaders are confident that they are going in the right direction and, thus, do not hesitate to take risks to accomplish their visions. They willingly tackle change—restructuring the organization, trying new ideas, and embracing innovation. TQM leaders are willing to invest a large amount of time and money up front for training. TQM leaders can withstand pressures for immediate profits from TQM techniques in order to ensure long-term change toward TQM principles.

5. *Exhibit an inspirational personal style.* Charismatic leaders exude a presence that draws their followers closer to them in a sort of personal magnetism. Followers identify with them and willingly look to them as role models. Charismatic leaders continually push followers to higher levels of ability and motivation.[9] TQM leaders must act as role models for employees in what they say, what they do, and what they value.

6. *Identify the benefits of following the vision.* Charismatics directly identify what the rewards for success are when the vision is met. The quest for the vision is thus worth the effort. TQM leaders can tie TQM principles of continuous improvement and customer satisfaction with long-term profitability, organizational growth, and individual employee growth.

Implications for the Reward and Recognition Process

These characteristic behaviors of charismatic leaders have several possible implications for the reward and recognition process in TQM.

1. *Frame the formal presentation of the award within the quality metaphors and stories of the organization.* An important part of the reward and recognition process is the formal presentation of the award, many times at a special dinner. Charismatic leaders can use their framing expertise to position the award within the organizational values of quality. They can use metaphors and stories in their presentation of the award to reinforce the importance of the award among the many symbols of quality of the organization.

2. *Create innovation awards.* Charismatics embrace change and will take risks to follow their vision. They can reinforce this risk-taking in their followers through awards that focus on innovations that individuals and teams have attempted. It is important to reinforce the attempt whether or not the innovation was actually successful in order to demonstrate to employees that innovation and the taking of the risks involved are central values of the organization.

3. *Create awards personally linked to the leader.* Employees identify closely with charismatic leaders. There is a kind of personal magnetism attracting the followers to the leader. This personal attraction can be incorporated in personal awards from the leader, such as a Special President's Award or the CEO's Quality Award. To reinforce the special personal nature of the award, a private meeting with the leader could follow the public presentation of the award.

4. *Link the reward and recognition process to the articulation of the vision.* A charismatic leader can clearly identify the rewards to

all who pursue the vision. Thus, it is important that the leader be actively involved in improving the reward and recognition process. The leader should meet with the reward and recognition team early in its work in order to restate the vision and delineate the rewards that follow, which will set the direction for the team's efforts.

THE ROLE OF COMPETITION

Competition is a controversial issue in TQM. Deming was obviously against it because it sets up the individual against the group. He believed that competition toward meeting personal goals replaces the cooperation and teamwork necessary for TQM to work.

At the same time, competition is a central value in U.S. culture. After all, the free market is based on the concept of open competition among firms. Not surprisingly, many firms now successfully practicing TQM did not originally embrace quality improvement. They balked at the high initial start-up costs of training and did not relish the organizational structural and cultural changes required. They were forced, however, to acknowledge the importance of continuous quality improvement because they were losing market share to competitors in the marketplace who were already developing TQM efforts.[10]

Moreover, competition is an effective motivational principle. In reinforcement theory, the value of rewards can be enhanced by offering them in a competitive environment, such as a game.[11] In goal setting, competition can offer challenge as well as provide feedback in meeting goals.[12] Indeed, an examination of several of the organizations cited in chapter 4 shows that competition is part of their reward and recognition process.

Therefore, competition cannot be stamped out as Deming would perhaps wish. It is important, however, that competition be managed effectively in the reward and recognition process. There are several points to keep in mind.

1. *Create a nonzero sum reward environment.* Many traditional competitive approaches assume a zero sum game. There has to be a winner, who gains at the expense of losers. This is what Deming correctly objected to. Competition does not have to imply winners and losers, however. If the reward and recognition system is being continuously improved, there should be an ever-larger number of rewards and awards for which to strive.

Everyone can compete and theoretically win. Thus, there do not have to be losers. Rather, there is a win-win environment. The competition is toward continuously improving—the individuals and the teams continuing to do better than they have before.

2. *Ensure that rewards are not concentrated on a few.* It is important to monitor the reward and recognition process to ensure that the same individuals and teams do not always win the same awards. Such concentrated rewards lose their value. Why should most employees compete for rewards and awards that the same few constantly win? Continuously adding to the rewards and awards available will lessen this possibility.

3. *Continuously change the focus of some awards.* In an environment with a constant number of awards with well-defined criteria for winning them, some individuals and teams will evolve a well-polished set of procedures that will guarantee winning the award in its present form. In other words, there may be tried and true methods for winning these awards. This, of course, locks the organization into certain courses of action for achieving quality and does not reinforce change or innovation. Such a scenario can be eliminated by continuously changing the focus of at least some of the awards. The reward and recognition team can identify these "variable" awards and then either write general guidelines that may be fulfilled a number of different ways, or publicize different emphases from year to year.

THE ROLE OF FEDERAL AND STATE AWARDS

There are a number of federal and state awards that recognize quality and initiative in organizations. Some firms actively set out to win these awards. They view the awards as a company-wide recognition of quality excellence. Other firms do not try to compete directly, but use the award guidelines as benchmarks for evaluating their quality progress. These awards can thus directly influence the reward and recognition process of the organization.

Baldrige Award

The Baldrige Award has the status of the national quality award. The seven criteria that companies must meet to win the award are described in chapter 1. They are summarized here with the weighting of each in the overall decision.

1. Leadership (10 percent)
   - Senior executives visibly involved in quality activities
   - All levels of management actively involved in quality

2. Information and analysis (7 percent)
   - Specific quality measures
   - Data collected on customers, processes, suppliers
   - Benchmark data on competitors

3. Strategic quality planning (6 percent)
   - Quality and customer orientation in strategic plans

4. Human resource utilization (15 percent)
   - Employee involvement and empowerment
   - Extensive training on quality improvement
   - Compensation plans reward quality efforts

5. Quality assurance and products and services (14 percent)
   - Product design reflects customer requirements
   - Operations involve continuous quality improvement
   - Improvement efforts for supplier quality

6. Quality results (18 percent)
   - Steady and continuous improvements documented
   - Firm is near top of market

7. Customer satisfaction (30 percent)
   - Measures of customer requirements
   - Continuous improvement of customer evaluation

Competition for the Baldrige Award is spirited. Hence, winning the award is highly motivating for companies. Moreover, surveys show that U.S. firms believe that the award promotes quality awareness as well the sharing of quality information.[13] But, there is another side. Some critics contend that some companies set their sights and their resources (and their TQM programs) toward the singular goal of winning the Baldrige Award. The award thus becomes an end rather than a recognition of companies' efforts toward continuous quality improvement. And, some companies who have won the award have later had financial problems, such as the Wallace Company, a petrochemical service supplier. It is still unclear whether the

Wallace Company, a relatively small firm, focused too many of its resources toward winning the award, whether it spent too much money giving presentations about the award after it was won, or whether the downturn of the oil industry was the major factor in the company's decline.[14]

State Awards

A recent survey showed that 35 states have a quality award program. These awards vary widely from quality awards to productivity awards to awards for team efforts.[15] A good example is the New York State Excelsior Award. Developed by a coalition of companies, organized labor, the public sector, and the education sector, the award recognizes quality excellence in private firms, government agencies, and education. Each subsequent year's applicants must at least meet the standards of the previous year's winners.[16]

Researchers have not been tracking the progress of state award winners like they have for the Baldrige Award. Therefore, we have little data on the award's subsequent effects on the winners. We should caution again, however, that a number of these state awards like the New York Excelsior Award are designed to be highly competitive. Organizations should consider at length what is their real motivation for pursuing such awards—winning, competing, impressing their customers, or evaluating their quality progress.

Implications of Federal and State Awards for Reward and Recognition

1. *Collect information on these awards.* Gathering award information can be considered part of the data collection process inherent in TQM. Gathering data on a number of awards allows the organization to pursue, if it wishes, awards that fit its circumstances.

2. *Benchmark award winners.* Benchmarking the successful efforts of other TQM organizations is an established means of gathering new ideas that the firm can try out on its own. Likewise, gathering information on award winners should yield ideas that have been successfully tested through the award competition process.[17]

3. *Benchmark award criteria.* The reward and recognition team of the organization can derive new ideas from award criteria. For example, suggestions for meeting criterion 4.4 of the Baldrige Award, which deals with employee performance and recognition, include showing employee involvement in constructing performance measures and showing timely feedback on employee efforts. In addition, part of each employee's compensation should be based on achieving quality goals. Recognition programs should be based on quality performance rather than on traditional data, such as safety records, work seniority, or sales figures.[18]

4. *Keep the award competition in perspective.* The ultimate goal of the organization is not winning awards but is continuous quality improvement. Winning the award (or simply competing for the award) can be one of many means, including customer data and SPC tools, used to evaluate the company's progress in its TQM efforts. Diverting the resources of the organization toward the singular goal of winning the award, however, is counterproductive.

WORK FORCE DIVERSITY

Diversity is an important issue in today's work force.[19] Originally focused on race, ethnicity, and gender, diversity now also includes work background, family background, education, physical abilities (or disabilities), and religious beliefs.[20] Indeed, work force diversity is now viewed as an environment of mutual respect, acceptance, and teamwork that mirrors the community and the customer base.[21] Two winners of the Baldrige Award have focused on diversity efforts in relation to their TQM programs.

Two Illustrations

Motorola. Motorola, a 1988 winner of the Baldrige Award, emphasizes employee diversity. In 1990 Motorola decided it was not in a position to attract the best and brightest as the U.S. work force demographics changed. It found that women and minorities were not well represented in management. In order to address these problems, Motorola set parity goals for placing women, African Americans,

Hispanics, and Native Americans at each level of management. Ultimately its goal is to have its work force reflect the gender and racial mix of the United States in the twenty-first century.

To accomplish this goal, Motorola targets recruiting toward diverse applicant groups. In addition, it has programs for management development of women and minorities, for helping women employees balance work and family life, for outreach to diverse groups in the community, and for scholarships. To show its commitment to the management of diversity, Motorola named the CEO as the corporate champion for diversity. As a consequence, Motorola has won a number of awards including the U.S. Secretary of Labor Opportunity 2000 Award and was named one of the top 100 companies by *Working Mothers*.[22]

Federal Express.   Federal Express won the 1990 Baldrige Award; it has been particularly attentive to Section 4 of the award: human resources development and management. Federal Express' focus is on improving the morale and well-being of its employees as internal customers. For example, Federal Express goes to great lengths to avoid employee layoffs. This is particularly important for the management of diversity because women and minorities, who many times are among the most recently hired, are particularly susceptible to layoffs (last hired, first fired). Further, Federal Express has a guaranteed fair treatment procedure that allows employees to appeal any issue to higher management. Employees can appeal decisions on promotions, compensation, benefits, and discipline through a formal review involving several management levels. Consequently, no employee issue has gone to third-party mediation or arbitration. In addition, Federal Express has standardized minimum job requirements in order to guarantee fair assessment of qualifications of job applicants.[23]

Advantages of Work Force Diversity for TQM

Work force diversity can provide several unique advantages for the TQM program.

1. *Widely diverse skills, knowledge, and experience.* Successful TQM depends on a multiskilled work force. Diverse employee groups possess a diversity of acquired work skills, knowledge of products and processes, and experience with work techniques. Further, their diverse backgrounds present a wide range of aptitudes for skills training, which is so important to TQM.

2. *Diverse inputs into quality teams.* TQM relies on cross-functional quality teams to monitor processes, identify problems, and arrive at solutions. Diverse work force representation on these teams can provide additional perspectives on defining the problem, approaches to the problem, and arriving at possible solutions.

3. *Input for TQM tools.* A diverse work force can enhance the use of TQM problem-solving tools, such as cause-and-effect diagrams, flowcharts, Pareto charts, and brainstorming. For example, research has shown that heterogeneous groups (members with different needs, personalities, orientation, and background) produce high-quality problem solving because they stimulate each other's abilities. Moreover, heterogeneous groups are particularly effective on complex tasks that require diverse problem-solving approaches, which directly describes many quality problems.[24] In the TQM setting, then, diversity as well as cross-functionality can improve quality teams.

4. *Diversity as a key to meeting customer needs.* Ultimately, the customer drives the TQM effort; customer needs define quality for the TQM organization. A diverse work force has a larger representation of the diverse types of customers many U.S. businesses serve. Such a work force will better know and understand the needs of a diverse customer base.

   Customers may feel more comfortable, and hence better served, if they see company employees similar to them. Further, if they have particular needs, such as language translations or knowledge of ethnic customs, workers of the same ethnic group may be the only employees who could fulfill this need. For example, US West focuses on Hispanic resource groups to help it understand and service the Hispanic market in the Southwest.[25]

Implications of Using Work Force Diversity to Improve TQM

1. *Strive for diverse employee membership on quality teams including the reward and recognition team.* When an organization sets up quality teams, it should look to the diversity of employee backgrounds as well as cross-functionality in the composition of the teams. Employee diversity can then provide

expanded inputs into problems, including reward and recognition. Individuals from different backgrounds can identify a breadth of employee needs to be met with rewards and recognition and can suggest a number of ways of rewarding individual and team efforts.

At the same time, it must be recognized that individuals with diverse interests, values, and attitudes may not result in a very cohesive team. Team-building training is particularly important for allowing these different individuals to coalesce into a well-functioning team.

2. *Use employee diversity to better serve diverse customer markets.* A major advantage of a diverse work force is that it can relate better to the diverse customer base of many companies. TQM organizations should reward direct links between its employees and target customer groups. These employees can help to monitor the needs of these specialized customer groups (and devise new customer service awards for meeting these diverse needs). For example, US West encourages African American, Hispanic, Native American, and women's employee groups to participate in its Pluralism Calendar of Events.[26]

3. *Reward diversity.* Organizations can publicly recognize diversity in their quality teams. For example, Motorola publishes a booklet containing the pictures of members of the finalist teams in their Quality Olympics. Many of these successful quality teams contain a mix of individuals in terms of gender, race, and ethnicity.[27] Moreover, organizations can create diversity awards that recognize the unique contributions to the quality effort of employees of various backgrounds (for example, suggestions for improvements in product design or customer service that target certain customer gender, race, or ethnic groups).

CONCLUSIONS

We have looked at four important issues to be dealt with in TQM. First, what will be the role of charismatic leadership? Charismatic leaders articulate a vision and inspire their followers toward attaining that vision; they can have a strong influence on the reward and recognition process. Second, what will be the role of competition? Although TQM leaders like Deming downplay competition, U.S. culture as well as the free market thrives on competition. Moreover, managed competition can be a potent motivator. Third, what will be the role of formalized awards? TQM organizations must decide the part that these awards will play—as standards to strive for, as the ultimate awards in the reward and recognition process, or even as something to be avoided because they divert the organization away from its primary mission of serving its customers. Fourth, how does the issue of employee diversity meld with TQM and reward and recognition? TQM organizations can benefit from the rich backgrounds and customer knowledge of a diverse work force.

These are only four of many important issues. Organizations must benchmark not only practices of other organizations but must actively follow developments in TQM research. They should closely monitor information sources, such as the *Quality Management Journal*, the new research journal from ASQC written for quality practitioners. Organizations must keep attuned to cutting edge developments and not be content merely to copy the practices of successful TQM organizations.

NOTES

1. Gary Yukl, *Leadership in Organizations*, 2d ed. (New York: Academic Press, 1989).

2. Bernard M. Bass, *Leadership and Performance beyond Expectations* (New York: Free Press, 1985).

3. Karl W. Kuhnert, "Transforming Leadership," in *Improving Organizational Effectiveness through Transformational Leadership*, ed. Bernard M. Bass and Bruce J. Avolio (Thousand Oaks, Calif.: Sage, 1993), 10–25.

4. A couple of good descriptions of charismatic leadership are Bass, *Leadership and Performance beyond Expectations* and Robert J. House, "A Theory of Charismatic Leadership," in *Leadership: The Cutting Edge*, ed. J. G. Hunt and L. L. Larson (Carbondale, Ill.: Southern Illinois University Press, 1977), 189–207.

5. Dan Ciampa, *Total Quality* (Reading, Mass.: Addison Wesley, 1992).

6. Bruce J. Avolio, "The Alliance of Total Quality and the Full Range of Leadership," in *Improving Organizational Effectiveness through Transformational Leadership*, ed. Bernard M. Bass and Bruce J. Avolio (Thousand Oaks, Calif.: Sage, 1993), 121–45.

7. Jay A. Conger, "Inspiring Others: The Language of Leadership," *Academy of Management Executive* 5 (February 1991): 31–45.

8. Avolio, "Alliance of Total Quality."

9. Ibid.

10. For descriptions of these firms, see Mary Walton, *The Deming Management Method* (New York: Putnam, 1986) and *Deming Management at Work* (New York: Putnam, 1990).

11. Fred Luthans and Robert Kreitner, *Organizational Behavior Modification and Beyond* (Glenview, Ill.: Scott, Foresman, 1985).

12. Gary P. Latham and Edwin A. Locke, "Goal Setting—A Motivational Technique that Works," *Organizational Dynamics* (Autumn 1979): 68–80.

13. Uly S. Knotts, Leo G. Parrish, and Cheri R. Evans, "What Does the U.S. Business Community Really Think about the Baldrige Award?" *Quality Progress* 26 (May 1993): 49–53.

14. Robert C. Hill and Sara M. Freedman, "Managing the Quality Process: Lessons from a Baldrige Award Winner, a Conversation with CEO John W. Wallace," *Academy of Management Executive* 6 (February 1992): 76–88.

15. Karen Bemowski, "The State of the States," *Quality Progress* 26 (May 1993): 27–36.

16. David B. Luther, "How New York Launched a State Quality Award in 15 Months," *Quality Progress* 26 (May 1993): 38–43.

17. Shari Cauldron, "Keys to Starting a TQM Program," *Personnel Journal* (February 1993): 28–35.

18. Nicholas Leifeld, "Inside the Baldrige Award Guidelines—Category 4: Human Resource Development and Management," *Quality Progress* 25 (September 1992): 51–55.

19. Stephen B. Knouse, Paul Rosenfeld, and Amy Culbertson, *Hispanics in the Workplace* (Newbury Park, Calif.: Sage, 1992); Marilyn Loden and Judy R. Rosener, *Workforce America* (Homewood, Ill.: Irwin, 1991).

20. "White, Male, and Worried," *Business Week* (31 January 1994): 50–56.

21. Shari Caudron, "US West Finds Strength in Diversity," *Personnel Journal* (March 1992): 40–44.

22. James Donnelly, *The Quality of People at Motorola* (Schaumburg, Ill.: Motorola, 1992).

23. Christopher W. L. Hart and Christopher E. Bogan, *The Baldrige* (New York: McGraw-Hill, 1992).

24. Andrew J. Szilagyi and Marc J. Wallace, *Organizational Behavior and Performance,* 5th ed. (Glenview, Ill.: Scott, Foresman, 1990).

25. Caudron, "Strength in Diversity."

26. Ibid.

27. Motorola, *Total Customer Satisfaction Team Competition Criteria* (Schaumburg, Ill.: Motorola, 1992).

Part III

Summing Up

Chapter 8

Continuous Improvement of the Reward and Recognition Process

Since TQM is a continuous push for improvement, the management system must itself continuously push, prod, encourage, praise, and reward.
—Richard J. Schonberger, "Total Quality Management Cuts a Broad Swath through Manufacturing and Beyond"

The purpose of this chapter is to integrate the material from the previous chapters around the central TQM theme of continuous improvement—in this case, continuous improvement of the reward and recognition process. First, we look at the TQM organizational structure supporting the reward and recognition effort. Next, we identify behavioral concepts to incorporate in designing an effective reward and recognition program. Then, we look at various types of reward and recognition that apply to internal customers (individual employees, teams, and managers) and to external customers. Next, we summarize principles to keep in mind for improving existing programs and implementing new programs in the reward and recognition process. Finally, we look at possible barriers to effective reward and recognition that might have to be addressed.

SUPPORTING ORGANIZATIONAL STRUCTURE

From chapters 1 and 2 we saw that there are two important TQM teams for the reward and recognition process.

TQM Steering Committee

The TQM steering committee, composed of top managers, sets the direction of the organization's TQM effort through the strategic plan.

It charters the major process teams, including the reward and recognition team. Very importantly, it allocates resources for the operation of the major processes and controls the expenditures. Therefore, through the strategic plan, the steering committee should recognize the importance of the reward and recognition process and allocate funds for various types of rewards and recognition, such as awards and formal award presentations.

Reward and Recognition Team

The reward and recognition team is a permanent quality team chartered by the steering committee to manage the reward and recognition process.

Charter. The purpose of the reward and recognition team should be continuous improvement of the reward and recognition process.

Team Membership. Membership should reflect all the major stakeholders in the reward and recognition process. The team should be cross-functional, comprised of representatives from different departments. In addition, a member of the steering committee should sit on the reward and recognition team for continuity. There also should be a TQM facilitator who is well trained in TQM tools. Ideally, there should be a human resources management facilitator who can help with interpersonal tools—teamwork, team role-taking, and various motivational principles that should be incorporated into rewards and awards.

Team Duties. Among the important team duties are the following:

1. *Analyze and monitor the reward and recognition process.* Using employee survey data and organizational procedures data, the team should diagram the reward and recognition process in depth. There should be flowcharts for the operation of each of the reward and award programs. As an illustration, Figure 8.1 shows a hypothetical flowchart for the process of nominating teams for an award, choosing the winning team, and presenting the award.

2. *Identify opportunities and problem areas.* Based on its analysis of the reward and recognition process, the team should identify opportunities for improvement as well as problem areas and should charter temporary teams to address these situations. For

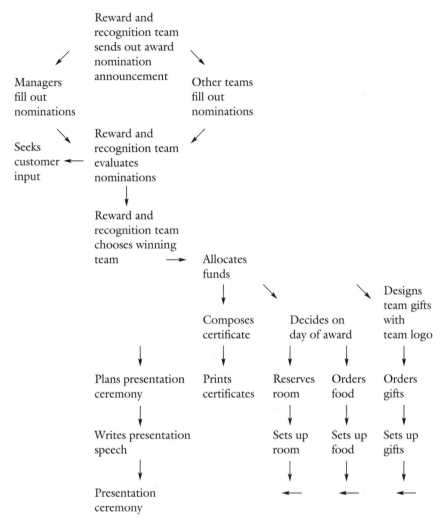

FIGURE 8.1. Hypothetical flowchart of a team award process.

example, Figure 8.2 is a hypothetical Pareto chart of components that customers rate as important for good customer service. These data could present an opportunity for refining a customer service award. If we were to use these data as criteria for such an award, they would show that problem solving is the most important criterion to customers and should be weighted the highest in the award, while sales of accessories during a service call is least important and should be weighted little, if at all, in the award.

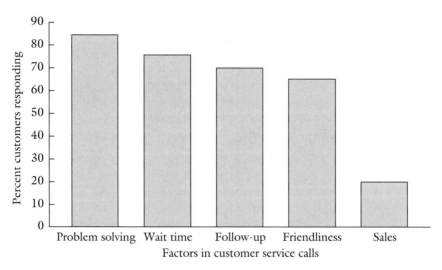

FIGURE 8.2.   Hypothetical Pareto chart of service factor importance to customers.

Figure 8.3 presents a hypothetical run chart of types of nominators for organizational awards (nominations by managers, other teams, and customers). The chart identifies a potential problem. Not all categories are nominating at the same rate. Managers may perhaps be overnominating, because they are using the awards process for their own ends (for example, "If you do what I want, I'll nominate you for more awards" or "I'll nominate everybody then nobody will be angry"). Or perhaps teams and customers are undernominating because there are obstacles in the nomination process that dissuade them from participating in the process. Further data gathering and analysis would be needed to pinpoint the problem and identify possible solutions.

3. *Benchmark other organizations.* From chapter 7 we saw that it is important that the team continually collect data from other organizations on effective and innovative reward and recognition programs. In addition, the team should keep abreast of state and national quality awards that could provide criteria for evaluating reward and recognition programs.

To illustrate these points, Figure 8.4 presents the charter and mission, duties, philosophy, and system design plan of StorageTek's Rewards and Recognition Team.[1]

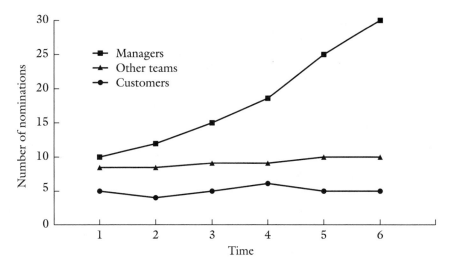

FIGURE 8.3. Hypothetical run chart of award nominations by nominator type.

Charter and Mission:

The charter and mission of the Rewards and Recognition Team is to determine the most effective methods for rewarding and recognizing employees for their involvement and contributions to StorageTek success and to revise the performance appraisal process to reinforce the values of quality, teamwork, and participative management.

Roles

- Definition of the rewards and recognition philosophy to support StorageTek strategic goals and Excellence Through Quality
- Identification of system process improvements to support StorageTek cultural changes
- Development of the rewards and recognition product line
- Development of the road map and communication plan
- Sponsorship of pilots to evaluate progress against the rewards and recognition plan
- Ongoing review of the implementation plan

Philosophy

Rewards and recognition can be powerful motivators of behavior. A solid direction for all locations worldwide and a corporate set of values tied to proper motivation are critical in developing the full potential of the work

Continued on next page

FIGURE 8.4. Directions of StorageTek's Rewards and Recognition Team. Source: StorageTek. Reprinted with permission.

force and in achieving ultimate success for StorageTek. The direction of our worldwide plan and the corporate set of values are defined in the StorageTek Operating Principles, the StorageTek Strategic Plan, the Human Resource Strategic Plan and the Excellence Through Quality 5-Year Plan. This Rewards and Recognition system emphasizes TEAMWORK, PROCESS IMPROVEMENT, CORPORATE PROFITABILITY, AND INDIVIDUAL CONTRIBUTION.

Steps in Rewards and Recognition System Design
- Cross-functional input facilitated by Human Resources
- Evaluation of current programs for revision and/or inclusion in rewards and recognition
  - Total compensation concept
  - Base pay structure
  - Performance appraisal
  - Merit increases
  - Bonuses/MBOs
  - Outstanding Contribution Recognition Certificates
  - Recognition (noncash programs)
  - Equity participation (stock options)
  - Profit sharing
- Synchronization of rewards and recognition with overall quality thrust
- Benchmarking with other companies
- Development of the Corporate Rewards and Recognition Product Line
- Delivering the philosophy to the subsidiaries and assisting them in the development of a total rewards and recognition system appropriate to local needs and constraints

---

FIGURE 8.4—Continued

BEHAVIORAL CONCEPTS TO INCORPORATE INTO THE DESIGN OF REWARD AND RECOGNITION PROGRAMS

In chapters 2 and 3 we examined a number of behavioral concepts that the reward and recognition team should incorporate into a successful reward and recognition program.

1. *Contingency.* Rewards and awards should be conferred as immediately as possible to the accomplishments. Moreover, rewards should be associated with the TQM program. Formal presentations, dinners, and receptions can strengthen the association of the effort with the overall TQM philosophy of the organization.

2. *Reward value or valence.* Rewards and awards should be valued by individual employees and employee teams. Management does not always know what employees prefer. Active participation of employees in setting up the program is necessary.

3. *Empowerment.* Employees cannot participate effectively unless they are empowered. Empowerment means not only allowing employee participation in important decisions but also giving employees the tools to participate. These tools center on extensive training of job skills, TQM statistical techniques, and team building.

4. *Win–win philosophy.* There should not be a zero sum game mentality where employees believe that they must beat someone else to win the award. Neither should the same individuals nor groups win the awards continually. Rather, employees and teams should believe that they can earn these various rewards and recognition with hard work (that is, they believe in a strong instrumentality that success will bring rewards).

5. *Variety of rewards and awards.* To support a win–win philosophy there should be a sufficient number and variety of rewards and awards that can be earned by different individuals and teams. The reward and recognition team should be continually thinking up new awards and new variations on existing awards. There can be awards from important individuals (for example, President's Award), awards focusing on quality (for example, Quality Achievement Award), awards focusing on efforts (for example, Quality Innovation Award), and awards focusing on customer service (for example, Customer Satisfaction Award).

TYPES OF REWARD AND RECOGNITION FOR INTERNAL AND EXTERNAL CUSTOMERS

Table 8.1 summarizes how the reward and recognition team can integrate these various concepts into the reward and recognition process

TABLE 8.1.   Reward and recognition for internal and external customers.

Focus	Means of empowerment	Indicators of performance	Types of	
			Financial rewards	Recognition awards
Internal customer				
Individual employee	Skills training	Improvement suggestions, contributions to the team	Skill-based pay, bonuses for suggestions, advanced training	Training, suggestions, team contribution, customer satisfaction
Team	Team building, increased problem-solving responsibility	Improvement suggestions, problem solving	Gain sharing, bonuses for suggestions	Teamwork, suggestions, cooperation, customer satisfaction
Manager	Facilitator training, increased customer responsibility	Leadership, customer satisfaction	Bonuses for customer satisfaction	Leadership, customer satisfaction
External customer	Membership on teams, access to organizational communication and information	Feedback	Compensation for feedback	Satisfied customer

for each level of internal customer (individual employee, quality team, and manager) and of the external customer. In order to pursue rewards or awards, employees at each level of the organization must have some means of empowerment that can motivate better performance. According to expectancy theory, empowerment through increased training and responsibility should increase expectancy of success. According to the job characteristics model, empowerment should lead to greater skill variety and responsibility.

    Each level in turn has a performance level toward which reward and recognition programs can focus measures of success. In chapter 4 we saw a variety of financial rewards and recognition awards that can be available for each level. Such variety can satisfy valence (different preferences for reward) and can provide enough rewards to create a win–win situation.

Internal Customers

Individual Employees. At the individual employee level, empowerment occurs through skills training both on and off the job. Performance can then be measured through individual employee suggestions for improvement and individual contributions to team efforts. From a financial standpoint, individuals may be rewarded with skill-based pay and bonuses for improvement suggestions. Moreover, advanced training itself could serve as a reward. Various individual awards could include recognizing training accomplishments, number of improvement suggestions (recognizing effort), suggestions that are implemented, contributions to team efforts, roles taken on teams (for example, contributor, facilitator, expediter, socioemotional supporter), and customer satisfaction.

Quality Team. At the quality team level, empowerment can occur through team-building training and through increased responsibility for solving quality problems. Team performance can be indicated by improvement suggestions implemented and problems solved. Financial rewards can take the shape of gain sharing of cost savings or procedural efficiencies derived from suggestions and team bonuses for improvements. Team awards could include teamwork awards, team suggestion awards, awards for cooperative efforts with other teams, and, of course, awards for satisfied customers.

Managers. Managers can be empowered through facilitator training where they learn to help teams solve problems and learn to coach people rather than direct them. In addition, managers can be given more direct responsibility for meeting customer demands. Managerial performance focuses on leadership of the TQM effort through role modeling, empowering individuals and teams, and inspiring employees to strive for quality improvement. Measures of managerial performance should directly reflect customer satisfaction. Managers can be financially rewarded through bonuses for improved levels of customer satisfaction.

Managerial awards can include leadership awards for role modeling, empowerment activities, and inspirational efforts. In addition, managers can win awards for satisfied customers.

External Customer

One level that most organizations have largely ignored is reward and recognition for the external customer. If quality is ultimately defined by customer satisfaction, then the customer as an integral part of the organization should be rewarded accordingly. Customers can be empowered to contribute to the organization through allowing them to sit on quality teams. In addition, customers should have access to organizational communication through linkage to electronic communication (for example, e-mail) and organizational databases (for example, research and development and product design programs). Customer performance for the organization is measured through customers' feedback on their own satisfaction with organization efforts. External customers can be rewarded financially through some type of compensation for feedback (for example, direct payments or rebates). External customers should also be allowed to win awards, such as the Most Satisfied Customer Award.

PRINCIPLES FOR CONTINUOUS IMPROVEMENT OF REWARD AND RECOGNITION

As the reward and recognition team looks to improve existing programs and implement new programs, it should keep in mind a number of tested principles that have been identified throughout this book for producing effective reward and recognition programs.

1. *The system is simple to understand and use.* Elaborate procedures to follow, forms to fill out, and levels of review ensure that the program will not work. Simple and direct procedures, forms, and review are more effective.

2. *Performance standards focus on customer satisfaction.* Chapter 5 showed that there can be multiple performance standards and multiple performance evaluators, but the customer must still be the ultimate focus. Performance standards that are met to earn

the reward or award must emphasize improving customer satisfaction.

3. *There is strong leadership.* Chapter 6 argued that leaders must address employee performance through an external attributional (systems-oriented) framework, while chapter 7 examined how the charismatic leader can affect the reward and recognition process. Managers must exhibit strong leadership in the process to produce a perception in the organization that reward and recognition programs are important, effective, and fair.

4. *Employees participate in setting up the program.* Employees know what types of rewards and awards they prefer. And, they have a pretty good idea of what types of recognition are lacking in the system. Employee participation should also motivate employees to work with the system to ensure its fairness and effectiveness.

5. *There is open communication.* Open communication means that employees know what the criteria for the reward and recognition programs are and how to achieve them. There are no secret agendas or hidden candidates. Open communication ensures that employees share ideas and information in order to improve the reward and recognition system.

6. *There is recognition for good efforts as well as accomplishments.* One of the basic problems of merit pay systems is that they focus on results only, not good efforts. Employees are reinforced for production quantity rather than good ideas. There should be at least some awards that are given for good ideas, for innovative thinking, for teamwork, for small wins as well as big accomplishments.

POSSIBLE BARRIERS TO EFFECTIVE
REWARD AND RECOGNITION

We must realize that reward and recognition, like any other TQM process, faces possible barriers to success that must be acknowledged and then dealt with.

1. *Time.* Serving on the reward and recognition team takes time. In addition, the reward and recognition work required between

meetings takes time (for example, collecting award data, investigating the cost of awards and ceremonies, organizing presentations, and evaluating candidates for awards). There must be rewards and recognition for the work put in by the reward and recognition team members.

2. *Cost.* Pay raises linked to quality improvement efforts can be expensive. Cost savings may take some time before there is a payback for raises. In addition, some pay variations, like skill-based pay, do not create immediate results. Consequently, budgeting for TQM reward costs like pay raises must be realistic and must have a longer time frame than other activities.

3. *Lack of culture change.* If the organization adopts a TQM program but organizational culture still rewards individual productivity gains and pits individuals against one another in competitive situations, then the reward and recognition program will have no credibility. Top management must emphasize that it is now rewarding quality improvement, customer service, and teamwork, and managers must follow through.

4. *Resistance to change.* Top management may try to change the organizational culture toward TQM, but managers and employees may resist such change. The old ways may be deeply ingrained because many managers and employees received raises and promotions under the old ways. The new way will be different and will create uncertainty. Strong positive leadership can ease the transition. Management must remember that sometimes small steps are easier to make than giant strides.

5. *Timing of change.* Given the reality of resource constraints, many organizations cannot afford a simultaneous transformation of all their processes to TQM at once. Indeed, rapid sweeping change may actually cripple the organization. Instead there should be a planned and extended period of change. For example, many Baldrige Award winners did not immediately immerse themselves in TQM. Rather they quickly upgraded the systems already in place (training and communication) and then waited on the more extensive and costly changes (for example, team-based compensation) until there was stronger acceptance of TQM and sufficient resources were in place.[2]

6. *Merging different cultures.* If a successful TQM organization buys another company, the clash of cultures may cause tempo-

rary problems with the TQM efforts. But if the program is effective, the problems may decline in a relatively short time. For example, when Federal Express, a Baldrige Award winner, acquired Tiger International, quality indicators declined initially. Federal Express was able to return to previous quality levels in eight months.[3]

7. *Hokey recognition programs.* Unfortunately, some recognition programs treat employees like children who can be satisfied with little trinkets.[4] Employees in these programs become tired of the coffee mugs, balloons, and gift certificates. This may well indicate that management believes it knows what employees want but has not solicited their input. Employees must be actively involved in designing the recognition programs.

8. *Rewarding TQM practices rather than customer needs.* Some organizations may focus on rewarding the extent to which TQM practices are visible and lose sight of their basic purpose of satisfying customer needs through continuous improvement. Such organizations may reward managers for how many quality teams they set up, reward quality teams for how many charts they produce, and reward individual employees for how many TQM videos they watch. To combat these tendencies, there has to be continuous reinforcement of the idea that the customer is the reason that the business exists and customer service is ultimately what is being rewarded.

CONCLUSIONS

Reward and recognition is an important process that requires management like any other process in the organization. A permanent reward and recognition team should oversee the reward and recognition process. This chapter reviews a number of principles that can be incorporated in managing reward and recognition. In the final analysis, however, each TQM organization must understand the unique characteristics of its own situation. Once the organization has a good handle on what it is, what its customers want, and where it is going, the organization must emphasize continuous improvement of its reward and recognition programs in order to best serve its employees as internal customers and its clients as external customers.

NOTES

1. StorageTek, *Rewards and Recognition Task Force Recommendations* (Louisville, Colo.: StorageTek, 1991).

2. Richard Blackburn and Benson Rosen, "Total Quality and Human Resources Management: Lessons Learned from Baldrige Award–Winning Companies," *Academy of Management Executive* 7, no. 3 (August 1993): 49–66.

3. Christopher W. L. Hart and Christopher E. Bogan, *The Baldrige* (New York: McGraw-Hill, 1992).

4. Ibid.

Chapter 9

Reward and Recognition: What We Already Know and What We Need to Know

When you have an answer for everything, you know you have stopped learning.

—Philip B. Crosby, *Quality Is Free*

As I was writing this book, one of the big leaders in TQM, Deming, suddenly died. I know his passing has caused a lot of people to stop and consider how TQM has progressed in the United States during the last decade and where it will go now that one of its leaders is gone.[1] I see an inevitable parallel to the effect of Sigmund Freud's death on psychology. Throughout his productive life, Freud continued to refine and further develop his theory of psychoanalysis. When he died in 1939, a strange thing happened: Freudian theory stopped evolving. We suddenly had orthodox Freudians who refused to allow any deviation from the writings of the master. Freudian theory started to fossilize in 1939 and is now thoroughly out of step with present-day psychology.

I would hope the same thing does not happen with TQM. I have seen Deming advocates who have treated his 14 principles as almost the Ten Commandments of TQM. Now that Deming is dead, will the Deming brand of TQM cease to evolve and become fossilized similar to Freudian theory? Will orthodox Deming followers refuse to allow any deviation from the principles put forth in *Out of the Crisis*, or will TQM continue to honor Deming's emphasis on continuous improvement in all things, including TQM itself? In short, Deming's death gives us a good reason to reflect on how far we have come in TQM and where are we going.

In this light, I would like to end this book by looking at what we already know about reward and recognition in TQM and what we still need to know in order to improve continuously.

143

REWARD AND RECOGNITION PROCESS

What We Already Know

1. *There are a variety of effective reward and recognition programs in place.* In chapter 4 we encountered a sampling of successful reward and recognition programs from organizations in several different sectors. These organizations used a variety of monetary rewards, such as skill-based pay, profit sharing, gain sharing, and bonuses. They also had a variety of recognition awards for skill acquisition, improvement suggestions, quality leadership, and solving quality problems.

2. *Rewards and recognition should be team driven.* Organizations are placing an increased emphasis on monetary rewards and recognition awards for team efforts in addition to individual efforts. Moreover, chapter 8 pointed out that a permanent reward and recognition team should be in place so that employees themselves can monitor and manage the reward and recognition process.

What We Need to Know

1. *What are the costs of the reward and recognition process?* When Deming was alive, he tended to downplay the costs of quality improvement as less important than long-term results.[2] For example, it was a given that TQM training costs would be high for companies implementing a TQM program, which has caused at least some companies to reconsider TQM.

    U.S. business, however, must run on budgets. And, the reward and recognition process should be costed out for budgeting like any other important process, such as production or marketing. Many companies have a handle on the direct costs of pay raises and bonuses and on the cost of engraving award plaques, but what are the indirect costs? How much do the award presentations cost the company—preparing speeches, writing articles for news releases, taking time away from work to attend the presentation? What are the costs of the reward and recognition team—costs of meeting times, evaluating award nominees, programming activities, and shopping for award plaques?

    Some human resources specialists, like Wayne F. Cascio, have developed cost-effectiveness procedures for human resources activities. For example, an analysis of the cost-effectiveness of training compares the costs of training (developing the program, materials, training time, and lost production time during training) to the return on training (time to reach competency, job performance, and work attitudes).[3]

2. *What are the cost savings (the return on investment) of the reward and recognition process?* We believe that reward and recognition results in higher job satisfaction, greater job involvement, and greater commitment to the organization. But what does that mean in dollars and cents? It is difficult to put a dollar value on improved attitudes. But we can attempt to identify the cost savings of the results of improved attitudes, such as higher productivity, lower absenteeism, and lower turnover. Again, Cascio may be helpful here. He has developed measures for calculating the cost savings due to decreases in absenteeism and turnover based on incremental improvements in attitudes.[4]

   Ultimately, what is the financial return of reward and recognition for quality—reduced errors, less waste, increased customer satisfaction? Such a question first requires that we identify how the reward and recognition process influences other processes, such as production and marketing. Then we must link costs and savings across these processes.

3. *What are the real problems with reward and recognition?* Companies like to publicize their successes but not their failures. We are seeing relatively little information on what does not work in the area of reward and recognition. Are there some programs that simply don't work anywhere? Are there certain types of employees who do not respond to certain types of reward and recognition? What are the organizational barriers to reward and recognition above and beyond what was mentioned in chapter 8? Are there some aspects of reward and recognition that cause managers particular troubles (for example, dealing with individuals or teams who do not win awards)?

MOTIVATION

What We Already Know

1. *There are several effective theories of motivation.* From chapter 3, expectancy theory shows that managers can increase motivation in TQM organizations through increasing the expectancy

of success (training and coaching), increasing the instrumentality that rewards are associated with successful performance, and increasing the valence (value) of rewards.

Reinforcement theory shows that managers can motivate through rewards that are contingent (immediately associated with performance) and valued (meet individual needs).

We already know that a large number of organizations use goal setting. And a large number of research studies shows that effective goals are specific, moderately difficult, and participative. Moreover, feedback directs performance toward goal attainment.

Finally, the job characteristics model shows that jobs themselves can be motivating if they offer variety, significance, responsibility, and feedback. Many basic and applied reward studies show that many organizations effectively use goal setting, behavior management (reinforcement theory), and job enrichment (job characteristics model).

What We Need to Know

1. *What is the best theory of motivation for TQM?* It is tempting to try to find the best theory of motivation for TQM. Unfortunately, motivation theorists have been unable to find a one best theory or even a good unifying theory for management in general. There is no reason to believe we would be more successful with TQM.

2. *What is the best theory given the situation?* A more productive direction is to determine what is best given the situation. In other words, it is better to take a contingency approach to TQM and motivation. Because so many firms already use some form of goal setting (MBO, strategic planning), goal setting might be a good first step in getting a handle on managing motivation.

   Expectancy theory and reinforcement theory are very individualized (different expectancies and rewards for different individuals) and require fairly good interpersonal relations between the supervisor and the employee. The supervisor must be able to directly influence expectancies through such means as coaching and must be able to influence directly rewards if they are to be contingent and valued. Therefore, an organization where relations between supervisors and employees are strained (for example, supervisors have had to lay off employees) or where supervisors do not come into frequent contact with employees (for example, employees at different sites) may have to work on better relations and more frequent contact before expectancy theory or reinforcement theory can be effective.

The job characteristics approach, which focuses on the job itself, may be most effective where the organization has gone through a recent reorganization and job definitions are more fluid as they are being refined. On the other hand, organizations with rigid job definitions, such as those found in a unionized company, may have difficulty applying the job characteristics model.

One important point here is that motivation and leader style are closely linked. In the search for the correct motivational theory for the situation, we should also look at what is the appropriate leader style, mentioned in chapter 7, to best carry out a certain motivational approach—transactional, charismatic, or participative?

PERFORMANCE EVALUATION

What We Already Know

1. *The performance evaluation system must support TQM.* The performance evaluation system must focus on evaluating the contributions to quality improvement that enhance customer satisfaction. That is what TQM is all about.

2. *The performance evaluation system must evaluate different levels of the organization on different criteria.* Chapter 5 showed that three important levels of evaluation are the individual, the team, and managers. Each of these levels should be evaluated on skills development, contributions, and improvements.

What We Need to Know

1. *How does performance evaluation evolve in the post-Deming era?* Deming was adamant that individual evaluation should be thrown out. In reality, many organizations will continue to evaluate individual performance. There will probably be a shift

toward a greater emphasis on TQM skill development, team contribution, and innovation. There also will be more emphasis on team evaluation by peers and managers.

There are persistent questions, however. Is there a best type of evaluation format—rating scales, checklists of TQM behaviors, or some new format? What role will performance evaluation play in organizational downsizing? Will individuals who do not acquire TQM-valued skills or who do not fit into teams be let go based on their TQM evaluations? What role will TQM performance evaluation play in the whole area of employee discipline and punishment? Will TQM evaluation, which stresses positive aspects, such as employee contribution and customer satisfaction, also be used to document unsatisfactory performance for firing? Or, will separate evaluation systems evolve for TQM and for discipline?

ORGANIZATIONAL ENVIRONMENT

What We Already Know

1. *Reward and recognition is an integral part of the organizational environment.* Chapter 2 showed that reward and recognition influences employee satisfaction with and commitment to the organization, which in turn should produce greater productivity and quality improvement, while reducing absenteeism and turnover.

2. *Reward and recognition is linked to organizational values and attitudes.* Chapter 6 described attribution theory as a vehicle for understanding how reward and recognition link to organizational values and attitudes. As the TQM organization develops, managers should change from an emphasis on personal attributions (seeing performance in terms of employee personality and motivation) toward situational attributions where the focus is on managing system causes of performance.

3. *Leadership is an integral part of the organizational environment.* Chapter 7 focused on transactional leadership for managing interpersonal relations and charismatic leadership for transforming the organization toward a vision of continuous quality improvement.

4. *Diversity is an integral part of the organizational environment.* Chapter 7 showed that work force diversity gives the organization a broader perspective on ways of solving quality problems. A work force composed of men and women, minorities, and individuals of different backgrounds offers unique means of understanding diverse customer target markets.

What We Need to Know

1. *What are organizational factors directly influencing the reward and recognition process?* Following the contingency approach, what is effective in one type of organization may not be effective in another. There are several variables that may influence what type of reward and recognition works and what does not.

   Organizational size may be a factor. Small firms may not need elaborate presentation ceremonies and formalized recognition practices if everyone knows everyone else well. Large firms may need more extensive recognition practices to reach everyone—formalized presentations, plaques on the wall, articles in company publications, and in-house message systems.

   Organizational technology may be a factor. High-tech firms may be able to use computers, local area networks, and television to place recognition in e-mail, electronic bulletin boards, and in-house broadcasts. Low-tech firms may be able to use something as simple as the occasion of a rest period during work to present an award.

   Type of employee also may be a factor. Firms that employ mostly highly educated and skilled individuals, like engineers, technicians, and people with a master's degree in business administration, may focus recognition on personal development (attending a professional conference or receiving advanced training as a reward). On the other hand, firms that employ largely blue-collar individuals (for example, heavy equipment assembly, freight hauling, and construction) might create quality teams around a sports theme. For them, effective reward and recognition may revolve around sports competition (for example, naming quality teams after sports teams) and sports-type awards (for example, baseball caps, trophies, and even sports events tickets as rewards).

2. *How does attribution theory influence organizational values?* Chapter 6 speculated that an external (situational) attributional value framework should change performance evaluation and leader behaviors toward an emphasis on managing system causes rather than personal causes of performance. What are further ramifications? Where does training fit into this scenario? TQM and job skills training may be seen as a system cause, but they also enhance personal development of individual employees, which may lead to a personal attribution of the employee.

   To what degree will individuals redefine their self-concept through their teams? Nobody believes that Americans in TQM organizations will become as group oriented as the Japanese, but at the same time the ambitious individual out to further his or her own career at the expense of others in the firm may have succeeded in the past, but will not fit into the TQM organization of the future.

3. *How does leadership fit with reward and recognition in the organizational environment?* We have already alluded to leadership styles and motivation. We know that there are many theories of leadership and leader style that are appropriate for different organizational environments. Charismatic leadership theory focuses on envisioning and personal magnetism. Everyone can't be charismatic, however. Charismatic leaders usually are most effective at the top of the organization. What leader behaviors are most appropriate for reward and recognition from first-level supervisors? Perhaps participative, transactional, or even technically oriented styles can be effective, depending on the type of organization and type of employee in the quality team.

   Are certain leader styles more appropriate for certain types of work? Probably authoritarian leaders would not fit into any type of TQM organization. But supportive leaders who focus on interpersonal rewards may be most effective in high-stress work environments, while participative leaders who allow extensive employee participation (who allow employees maximum leeway to create their own rewards and recognition) may be most effective in high-tech environments requiring highly skilled employees.[5]

4. *What are the ramifications of diversity and TQM?* On the one hand, work force diversity should produce broader perspectives on diverse customer needs. But at the same time, quality teams composed of diverse individuals with greatly differing values and attitudes may not be very cohesive. How does the organization which is committed to work force diversity fit its diverse workers into close-knit quality teams? A strong message from leaders that diversity and innovation go hand-in-hand helps. Extensive team-building training also helps. Rewarding employee acceptance of work force diversity helps further. Public recognition of the accomplishments of quality teams composed of individuals of differing gender, race, ethnicity, and age helps even more.

CONCLUSIONS

We have come a long way, but we have a long way yet to travel. There are few simple and direct answers for the many questions about reward and recognition raised in this chapter. We cannot definitely state what is the best type of reward or recognition to use, or what is the optimal motivational principle, or the best leader style, or even what organizational factors to consider in a good reward and recognition system.

Perhaps Deming did us a favor by not having a 15th principle on reward and recognition that says that reward and recognition must follow a certain form. There is a certain advantage to the absence of any such authoritative statement; we are free to mold reward and recognition to fit the needs of our employees, our organization, and, ultimately, our customers.

NOTES

1. See the special section of the March 1994 issue of *Quality Progress* that highlights Deming's contributions in several articles including "Gone But Never Forgotten," "Recollections about Deming," and "Recollections from Japan."

2. W. Edwards Deming, *Out of the Crisis* (Cambridge, Mass.: MIT Center for Advanced Engineering Study, 1986), 25.

3. Wayne F. Cascio, *Costing Human Resources: The Financial Impact of Behavior in Organizations*, 3d ed. (Boston: PWS-Kent, 1991).

4. Ibid.

5. I have borrowed the ideas of directive (authoritarian), supportive, and participative leader styles from Robert House's "A Path-Goal Theory of Leadership Effectiveness," *Administrative Science Quarterly* (September 1971): 321–39.

Suggested Reading

American Management Association. *Total Quality Management: A Special Report from Organizational Dynamics.* New York: American Management Association, 1992.

Bass, Bernard M. *Leadership and Performance beyond Expectations.* New York: Free Press, 1985.

Bass, Bernard M., and Bruce J. Avolio, eds. *Improving Organizational Effectiveness through Transformational Leadership.* Thousand Oaks, Calif.: Sage, 1993.

Belasco, James A., and Ralph C. Stayer. *Flight of the Buffalo: Soaring to Excellence, Learning to Let Employees Lead.* New York: Warner Books, 1993.

Cascio, Wayne F. *Costing Human Resources: The Financial Impact of Behavior in Organizations.* 3d ed. Boston: PWS-Kent, 1991.

Ciampa, Dan. *Total Quality.* Reading, Mass.: Addison-Wesley, 1992.

Crosby, Philip B. *Quality Is Free.* New York: McGraw-Hill, 1979.

Crosby, Philip B. *Let's Talk Quality.* New York: McGraw-Hill, 1989.

Dean, James W., and James R. Evans. *Total Quality: Management, Organization, and Strategy.* Minneapolis, Minn.: West, 1994.

Deming, W. Edwards. *Out of the Crisis.* Cambridge, Mass.: MIT Center for Advanced Engineering Study, 1986.

Evans, James R., and William M. Lindsay. *The Management and Control of Quality.* 2d ed. Minneapolis, Minn.: West, 1993.

Golomski, William A., ed. *Quality Management Journal* (October 1993 to present).

Hackman, J. Richard, and Greg R. Oldham. *Work Redesign.* Reading, Mass.: Addison Wesley, 1980.

Harrington, H. James. *The Improvement Process.* New York: McGraw-Hill, 1987.

Hart, Christopher W. L., and Christopher E. Bogan. *The Baldrige.* New York: McGraw-Hill, 1992.

Houston, Archester, and Steven Dockstader. *A Total Quality Management Process Improvement Model*, NPRDC-TR-89-3. San Diego, Calif.: Navy Personnel Research and Development Center, 1988.

Ishikawa, Kaoru, and David J. Lu. *What Is Total Quality Control? The Japanese Way*. Englewood Cliffs, N.J.: Prentice Hall, 1985.

Juran, J. M. *Juran's Quality Control Handbook*. 4th ed. New York: McGraw-Hill, 1988.

Juran, J. M. *Juran on Leadership for Quality*. New York: The Free Press, 1989.

Knouse, Stephen B., Paul Rosenfeld, and Amy Culbertson. *Hispanics in the Workplace*. Newbury Park, Calif.: Sage, 1992.

Latham, Gary P., and Kenneth N. Wexley. *Increasing Productivity through Performance Appraisal*. 2d ed. Reading, Mass.: Addison Wesley, 1994.

Lawler, Edward E. III. *Strategic Pay: Aligning Organizational Strategies and Pay Systems*. San Francisco, Calif.: Jossey-Bass, 1990.

Lawler, Edward E. III, Susan Albers Mohrman, and Gerald E. Ledford. *Employee Involvement and Total Quality Management: Practices and Results in FORTUNE 1000 Companies*. San Francisco: Jossey-Bass, 1992.

Luthans, Fred, and Robert Kreitner. *Organizational Behavior Modification and Beyond*. Glenview, Ill.: Scott, Foresman, 1985.

Mawhinney, Thomas C., ed. "Special Issue on Organizational Behavior Management and Statistical Process Control: Theory, Technology, and Research." *Journal of Organizational Behavior Management* 9, no. 1 (1987): 1–156.

Pinder, Craig C. *Work Motivation*. Glenview, Ill.: Scott, Foresman, 1984.

Sashkin, Marshall, and Kenneth J. Kiser. *Total Quality Management*. Seabrook, Md.: Ducochon Press, 1991.

Steers, Richard M., and Lyman W. Porter. *Motivation and Work Behavior*. 5th ed. New York: McGraw-Hill, 1991.

Trice, Harrison M., and Janice M. Beyer. *The Cultures of Work Organizations*. Englewood Cliffs, N.J.: Prentice Hall, 1993.

Vroom, Victor H. *Work and Motivation*. New York: Wiley, 1964.

Walton, Mary. *The Deming Management Method*. New York: Putnam, 1986.

Walton, Mary. *Deming Management at Work*. New York: Putnam, 1990.

Weary, Gifford, Michael A. Stanley, and John H. Harvey. *Attribution*. New York: Springer-Verlag, 1989.

Yukl, Gary. *Leadership in Organizations*. 2d ed. New York: Academic Press, 1989.

Index